YOKO ONO
COLLECTOR OF SKIES

NELL BERAM & CAROLYN BORISS-KRIMSKY

AMULET BOOKS · NEW YORK

For Eva and Marlon, my favorite young artists —N. B.

For Eliot, Alyssa, Will, Benjamin, and Andrew —C. B. K.

Library of Congress Cataloging-in-Publication Data

Beram, Nell.
Yoko Ono : collector of skies / by Nell Beram and Carolyn
Boriss-Krimsky.
p. cm.
Includes bibliographical references and index.
ISBN 978-1-4197-0444-4 (alk. paper)
1. Ono, Yoko. 2. Artists—United States—Biography.
I. Boriss-Krimsky, Carolyn. II. Title.
NX512.O56B47 2013
700.92—dc23
[B]
2012011539

Text copyright © 2013 Nell Beram and Carolyn Boriss-Krimsky
Book design by Maria T. Middleton

Printed and bound in China
10 9 8 7 6 5 4 3 2 1

Amulet Books are available at special discounts when purchased in quantity
for premiums and promotions as well as fundraising or educational use.
Special editions can also be created to specification. For details, contact
specialsales@abramsbooks.com or the address below.

THE ART OF BOOKS SINCE 1949

115 West 18th Street
New York, NY 10011
www.abramsbooks.com

1

COLLECTING SKIES

(1933–1953)

"I was never able to get hold of my mother without touching her manicure and fur."

—YOKO ONO, 1973

PAGE VI East meets West: Yoko circa 1935, in a traditional Japanese kimono (left) and in a stylish European ensemble (right). These two styles reflect her mother's desire to expose Yoko to both Eastern and Western cultures.

Yoko and Keisuke were hiding in an abandoned building. Like many Japanese children, they had been evacuated from war-torn Tokyo and brought to the countryside. They were hungry. But Yoko was less distressed about her empty stomach than about her usually upbeat younger brother's listlessness.

"Let's create a menu, OK?" she said. "Think of the dinner you want to eat."

After some prodding, he offered, "I want ice cream."

"But that's a dessert," she said. "We should start with soup, of course."

Yoko goaded him some more, and together, lying on their backs and looking up at the ceiling, they created fantasy menus as though ideas alone could feed them. Through a crack in the roof, Yoko caught a glimpse of the blue sky, and at that moment she felt certain that everything would be all right.

It wouldn't be the last time the sky would provide comfort and imagination would seem to have the power to save her life.

NORMALLY, YOKO ONO was not a child who seemed in need of saving. Her family was wealthy and powerful, and her lineage included scholars, warriors, and rulers. But she never would have been born if Eisuke Ono and Isoko Yasuda hadn't done something unusual for Japanese people in the early 1930s: They married for love.

Yoko's father, Eisuke, came from a long line of scholarly samurai warriors. He could even claim to be the descendant of a ninth-century emperor. Eisuke's father was a Tokyo banker who, like Eisuke's mother, valued education. Their son earned advanced degrees in economics and math at Tokyo University. Eisuke's true passion, however, was music. He was

2

moved by Bach, Beethoven, Brahms, and some of the other composers of Europe—not the Eastern musicians he had grown up listening to.

Eisuke embarked on a professional career as a pianist. He was a favorite performer at social events in Karuizawa, a village in the mountains a hundred miles north of Tokyo, where his family—well-off but certainly not rich—had a summer home. Given Eisuke's good looks, smarts, and obvious talent, it was no wonder that young women considered him a catch.

Around Karuizawa, Isoko Yasuda was impossible to miss. She was exceptionally beautiful, fashionable, and wealthy. Her paternal grandfather, Zenjirō Yasuda, had been the founder of the prominent Yasuda Bank. Zenjirō was succeeded as head of the bank by Isoko's father, Zenzaburo. Practically everybody in Japan had heard of the Yasudas. Isoko could have married just about anyone she wanted to.

After Isoko and Eisuke began a romance, Eisuke's dream of furthering his musical career began to fall apart. Isoko had grown up like a princess, in an extravagant household with thirty-odd servants. She was chauffeured around in a private car and rewarded with diamonds just for getting good grades. Her parents didn't approve of their daughter, whose assets far exceeded Eisuke's, marrying a musician. It didn't help that he, like a small minority of Japanese, was Christian. The Yasudas were Buddhist.

In Japan, as in the West at that time, a married man was seen as the provider for the household, and a musical career didn't guarantee a good income. But in the end, it wasn't Isoko's parents who convinced Eisuke to give up his musical ambitions. After his father died, Eisuke learned from his will that he wanted his son to stop playing the piano and follow

Yoko was born into a wealthy family, but she didn't have everything: She didn't meet her father until she was two and a half years old.

in his footsteps by becoming a banker. Eisuke agreed—reluctantly—to give up music to honor his dead father's wishes and to please the parents of the woman he loved.

After Eisuke and Isoko wed, he moved into the dauntingly large Yasuda compound, where Isoko had been living, in the ancient city of Kamakura, which overlooked Tokyo. It was in

those palatial surroundings that Yoko came into the world one snowy night, on February 18, 1933. But Eisuke wasn't there for Yoko's birth. Two weeks earlier, he had been transferred from a bank in Tokyo to one in San Francisco. In Yoko's first memory of her father, he is a mysterious stranger looking out at her from a photograph. "My mother would show me his picture before bedtime and tell me, 'Say good night to Father.'"

Yoko didn't actually meet Eisuke until she was two and a half years old, when she and her mother traveled by ship to California to be with him. "My father looked like a tall American Indian chief," she said. "He stood straight; he was elegant and proud." But she didn't sense that he was happy to meet her.

It was in California that Yoko gave her mother a shock that would steer the way Isoko raised her daughter. While the Onos were in the dining room of a hotel near Yosemite National Park, where the family was taking in the sights, Yoko stood before some elderly women and, out of the blue, started singing Japanese children's songs.

Isoko was horrified by what she heard coming from her daughter's mouth. She considered these songs the music of commoners and therefore a sign of poor breeding. She knew that Yoko could have learned the songs only from her nannies back in Japan. Isoko vowed to send Yoko, once she was old enough, to Tokyo's best private schools, where the little girl would learn what her mother viewed as proper behavior.

In the spring of 1937, the family, which now included baby boy Keisuke, returned to Tokyo. Isoko and Eisuke had sensed that it was time. Japan was openly pursuing its ambition to become a world superpower by sending troops to China, a friend to the United States. This intrusion created anti-Japanese sentiment in America. Yoko's parents could feel it.

The family was now living in a Western-style mansion in Azabu, one of Tokyo's affluent residential districts. Isoko followed through on her pledge to give her daughter only the best by sending her to Jiyu Gakuen, a celebrated Tokyo school for girls that Isoko herself had attended as a child. Known for producing some respected Japanese musicians, the school taught even very young children piano, pitch, harmony, and composition. Yoko began at Jiyu Gakuen when she was only four years old—her age when she gave her first public concert, on piano. She had never been so nervous in her life. Performing didn't get easier right away. "I remember running offstage and throwing up after one concert," she recalled.

She liked learning about and writing music, though. One of the things she learned at Jiyu Gakuen was to listen to sounds in her environment. For homework she was asked to translate everyday noises, like street traffic or a bird's song, into musical notes.

But Isoko didn't think that Jiyu Gakuen was quite good enough for her daughter. The following year she sent Yoko to an even more prestigious school called Gakushūin. The school was located near Tokyo's Imperial Palace, where Japan's imperial family lived, and it accepted students only if they were related to the imperial family or to members of the House of Peers, part of Japan's parliament. Yoko's acceptance was guaranteed: Her grandfather Zenzaburo had been inducted into the House of Peers in 1915, long before she was born. She took her place among the other privileged children of royalty and government officials.

At Gakushūin, Yoko continued to learn about music. She wrote songs and created drawings to go with her melodies. She also wrote haiku, a form of Japanese poetry made up of

OPPOSITE This picture was taken in San Francisco circa 1935, not long after Yoko met her father, Eisuke, for the first time. Her mother, Isoko, was a very protective parent. Yoko recalled, "My attendants always carried absorbent cotton dipped in alcohol on an occasion like a family trip. They disinfected every place I was likely to touch on a train. That was because of my mother's partiality for cleanliness. Thus, I became sensitive to cleanliness too."

three nonrhyming lines that together usually contain exactly seventeen syllables. "People used to say, 'When Yoko takes steps, a poem comes out of her mouth as she stops,'" she said later.

EISUKE MARVELED AT Yoko's musical ability. He was happy to provide her with an extensive musical education that included private lessons. But Eisuke was inaccessible as a father, forever preoccupied with work even when he wasn't away on business (as he frequently was). "My father had a huge desk in front of him that separated us permanently," Yoko later wrote.

Her mother was a similarly elusive presence. Isoko was known for giving lavish Hollywood-style parties for Tokyo's glamorous social elite. "It was like having a film star in the house," Yoko said of her mother. When Isoko entertained, Yoko often watched from afar, usually attended by one of her nannies. She was enchanted by the scene—it was like some fairy-tale ball—but she knew that Isoko didn't want her in the picture. "My mother had her own life. She was beautiful and looked very young. She used to say, 'You should be happy that your mother looks so young.' But I wanted a mother who made lunch . . . and didn't wear cosmetics."

And she wanted one who didn't criticize her daughter's looks. Isoko would tell Yoko that she was "handsome" but "not pretty; pretty girls don't have those big [cheek]bones." For Yoko, this was particularly hurtful coming from someone who obviously put much stock in appearances.

Isoko excelled in many of the arts, especially painting and drawing, and she took the time to share her skills and techniques with Yoko. She once warned her daughter against marriage and motherhood, claiming that they had prevented her from having a career as a painter. "She was always ... intimidating because she was such a good painter," Yoko said. "When I was a little girl, and I had to do homework for a painting class, she'd say, 'No, no. Just wait, wait. Do it this way.' And one day, I had to take this piece of work to school that was [practically] done by her. I was feeling so embarrassed, but there was no choice but to take that painting to school. Everyone was saying, 'It's so good. I can't believe it's *so* good.'"

Like Eisuke, Isoko acknowledged Yoko's artistic talents, and like him, she raised their daughter from an emotional distance. She told her servants to let Yoko get up all by herself when she fell down—in hopes that the experience would make the little girl stronger and more independent. "I still remember ... several women in kimono staring at me without offering a hand while I was trying to get up from the ground," Yoko later wrote.

At Gakushūin, Yoko stood apart from other kids her age. Petite in comparison, she also appeared more mature and worldly than her peers. Most Japanese children were raised to act subservient out of respect for their elders at all times, even bowing before their teachers. Yoko was different. She was less afraid than her classmates to ask questions, sometimes even challenging her elders.

Her parents may not have anticipated this side effect of Yoko having lived in the United States, where adults often encouraged children to freely offer their opinions. Still, Isoko and Eisuke were determined that their daughter grasp the English language and be familiar with Western culture. This was important to many Eastern families, who saw knowledge of Western ways as a ticket to success. But that kind of success wasn't on Yoko's mind. "I was terribly lonely," she said. "At school ... I didn't have any friends."

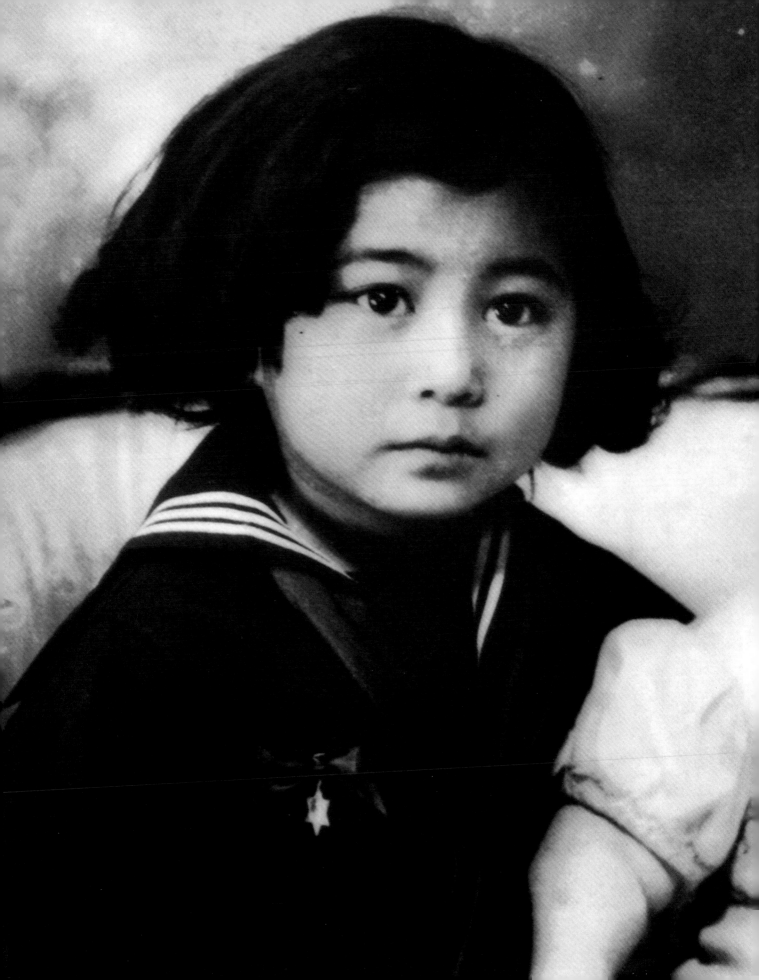

When she wasn't in school, Yoko was constantly in the company of servants and teachers: "There were several maids and private tutors beside me. I had one private tutor who read me the Bible and another foreign tutor who gave me piano lessons, and my attendant taught me Buddhism." At times she turned to her caretakers for friendship, comfort, even love—a risky proposition, considering there was no way of knowing how long they would be working for her parents. They were often let go quickly because Isoko had such high standards. When the servants left, Yoko feared that it was her fault.

Her intellectual needs were being met by instructors, her day-to-day needs by household staff. Yet Yoko still felt abandoned. She longed for her parents to spend more time with her. She later wrote of eating her meals alone: "I was told the meal was ready and went into the dining room, where there was a long table for me to eat at. My private tutor watched me silently, sitting on the chair beside me." Isoko forbade her from visiting the children of the servants, but at times, because she was desperate for someone to play with, Yoko would approach the daughter of one of her caretakers. When the surprised little girl realized that Yoko wanted to actually *play* with her, her reply was a submissive "I would do whatever you wish to, miss" or "What would you like to do, miss?"

EISUKE WAS WORKING for a bank in New York in 1940—a time of escalating tension between Japan and the United States. After Japan began aggressively mining China's natural resources in its attempt to become a world power, the United States had come to China's aid. Now many Americans were wondering if Japan would retaliate against the United States.

Meanwhile, in yet another part of the world, Germany's

chancellor, Adolf Hitler, was heading a murderous campaign to expand the German empire. His Nazi Party, which believed in the superiority of the German race, was singling out for death anyone who wasn't part of the white, Christian, able-bodied mainstream, including Gypsies, gays, the disabled, and, especially, Jews. The United Kingdom and France had already declared war on Germany. But Japan and Italy joined forces with Germany, and the three became known as the Axis powers. They pledged to support one another against their adversaries.

Because of this unrest, Isoko feared that the U.S. government would soon impose travel restrictions, which would mean that it might be years before she could see her husband again. So she bravely brought Yoko and her brother, Keisuke, by ship to California, and from there they took a train across America to New York. The Ono family set up house on Long Island, where Yoko went to public school and became fluent in English.

But a year later, in the spring of 1941, just as eight-year-old Yoko was flourishing academically and starting to make friends, Isoko decided that it was time for her and her children to sail back to Tokyo: She and Eisuke were certain that a war between Japan and the United States was imminent. Yoko, too, knew that something was brewing. Children in her own neighborhood were friendly to her, but if she went just a couple of blocks away, kids who lived there would throw stones at her simply because she was Japanese. She couldn't even escape from her race at the movies: "I remember being in film theaters where the baddies were always Asian. When the lights went up, I thought, am I [a baddie too]?"

Eisuke, who sailed home to Japan several weeks after his

family did, didn't stay put in Tokyo for long. He was soon sent to manage a branch of his bank in Japanese-occupied Hanoi, the capital of French Indochina (which later became Vietnam). Yoko disliked her father's absences, but she was used to them.

Yoko on an ocean liner to meet her father for the first time.

The United States was trying hard to stay out of the turmoil going on in the world. Aside from offering aid to China and refusing to give oil and other necessities to Japan, the country remained politically neutral. But on December 7, 1941, Japan attacked Pearl Harbor, a U.S. Navy base on the Hawaiian island of Oahu. Around twenty-five hundred servicemen and civilians were killed. The United States declared war the following day, joining up with the United Kingdom, the Soviet Union, and the other Allied nations working together to defeat the Axis powers. Young as she was, Yoko picked up on the fact that her parents didn't believe in war and thought that what Japan had done was unconscionable.

Initially, the Onos' wealth shielded them from the harsh realities of World War II, which included gasoline shortages and food scarcity. Many homes had no electricity or running water. Isoko had to let some of her servants go, but overall, the Ono family, which now included baby girl Setsuko, was beyond fortunate. Not only did the Onos have all the amenities of life, but they also had their very own bomb shelter in their expansive garden. The shelter contained enough food and water to enable the family to survive underground for days.

Isoko did as she would have during peacetime: She tried to give her children the best that money could buy. She enrolled Yoko in a Christian primary school in Tokyo called Keimei Gakuen, where the children were encouraged to speak English and study the Bible, although Yoko's parents continued to expose her to Buddhism as well. She received special treatment at school. She knew it wasn't fair that, because of who her parents were, she had advantages that other children didn't. But what could she do? She couldn't just stop being an Ono.

Keimei Gakuen was intended for Japanese children who had been educated abroad—children exactly like Yoko. But she still wasn't accepted by the other students. She later wrote, "I remember being called an American spy by other kids for not singing the Japanese national anthem fast enough."

It didn't help that her style of dress was unique, even among Tokyo's elite. Isoko had Yoko wear skirts and blouses cut in the American style. For a time Isoko even had Yoko's hair done in ringlets like the Hollywood child star Shirley Temple. Yoko's dramatic gestures and easy laughter, which were also associated with American ways, further set her apart from her peers.

Yoko saw herself as an outsider wherever she went, unsure of her identity—Christian or Buddhist? Easterner or Westerner?—or where she belonged.

Being uprooted meant having no long-standing friends, so Yoko spent much of her time reading, writing stories and poems, drawing, practicing the piano, and just letting her imagination wander. "I knew what I was doing when it came to art from the word *go*," she said later. "I think that had a lot to do with the fact that I was shy and art allowed me to communicate in a way that didn't require so much courage."

As the war raged on, the Onos' money could no longer insulate them. Yoko and her family often had to hide during the air raids. "In the middle of the night, we were woken up to go down into the shelter while the B-29s firebombed our city," she later wrote. "It was frightening to see fire burning down the houses around us . . . The food was scarce. I remember we were always hungry. It was not just food. There was a shortage of everything, even toilet paper." When the frequency of the American planes' bombings got to be too much, Keimei Gakuen, which had been within walking distance of the Onos' home, moved out of the beleaguered city. Isoko pulled Yoko out of school because she feared for her daughter's safety.

One day in March 1945, when she was walking in her garden, Isoko found a piece of scrap metal from a bomb—a souvenir of the previous night's air raid. She made a decision: It was time to join the thousands of others who were fleeing the city. She sent Yoko, along with Yoko's younger siblings and the children's nanny—all of the Onos' other servants had been forced into military service—by train to a farming village in the country, south of Karuizawa, where she hoped they would be safe. Isoko joined them a few days later.

The family took up residence in a small farmhouse in a cornfield. From Tokyo, Isoko had bought the land and paid a farmer to build a house on it, but he hadn't finished the roof by the time the Onos arrived, and he never did. Their problems didn't end there. Searching for something to eat, the Onos were treated with hostility by the farmers, who hardly had enough food for themselves, let alone to share with Yoko and her family, whom they regarded as stuck-up rich people.

"The farm folks hated the city folks, saying that they had fun all their lives in the city and now they're crawling to the farmers for food," Yoko said. "Our money couldn't buy food. It all depended on the farmers' whims. Sometimes you would give expensive jewelry in exchange for a bowl of rice, and still they would skip on the deal." Yoko had her own tormentors. "The farm boys threw stones at me . . . My mother said, 'You can write about all this one day when it's over.' That was my one hope amidst the terrible days of war. 'One day I'll write about all this.' By saying that, I felt better."

Yoko and her family survived by their wits and determination. "I couldn't sleep," she said. "I went through a period when I was really skin and bones." The nanny had better luck getting food than the Onos did because she was of the farmers' social class, but it wasn't enough. The Onos piled their belongings into an old wheeled cart and went from farm to farm, foraging for food and selling their clothing, beloved possessions, and other items. For a large sack of rice they traded Isoko's lovely hand-carved sewing machine, which had belonged to her father. To Yoko this didn't seem like a fair trade at all, yet she and her family had no other option, she realized, if they wanted to survive.

The nanny was finally summoned to military service. Isoko, who hadn't intended to leave her ladylike behavior in the city, now had the undignified task of carrying young Setsuko on her back. At one point Isoko pulled their cart from a muddy rice paddy—a humiliation for a woman whose hands had never known manual labor. Yoko helped her family as well as a child could. "I found this farmhouse, and there was a pile of potatoes on the floor," she said. "I filled my knapsack with them—my knapsack was as large as I was—and it was so heavy I had to go two steps and rest, two steps and rest, all the way back to my village."

Isoko traveled back and forth to Tokyo by train to tend to various matters at home. She also hoped to receive word from her husband or his colleagues regarding his whereabouts: The Allied forces had taken Hanoi, and the family had no way of knowing if Eisuke was dead or alive. Yoko was, of course, petrified at the prospect of losing her father, but she understood that her mother frowned on dramatic displays of emotion. Besides, she couldn't let on to her brother and sister that she was worried. Whenever Isoko went to Tokyo, she left twelve-year-old Yoko in charge of her siblings.

Making matters worse, Isoko had enrolled Yoko and her brother in a rural school where the other kids hassled them because their big-city mannerisms and Western ways made them stick out. Some of the children teased Yoko for "smelling like butter"—a reference to the fact that she had presumably been Americanized right down to the food she ate. Keisuke became so upset by the taunting that he stopped attending school. But Yoko stuck with it. In braids and trousers and with a knapsack on her back, she now looked more like a peasant than like a privileged city girl, but she held her head high.

THE WAR CAME to an end the way wars often do: catastrophically. On August 6, 1945, the United States dropped an entirely new and unimaginable weapon—the atomic bomb—on Hiroshima, a major urban center in southern Japan that provided supplies for the military. Instantly, more than eighty thousand people were killed. (Tens of thousands more would die from injuries and radiation poisoning in the months and years to come.) Three days later, the United States dropped another atomic bomb, this time on Nagasaki, a small port city south of Hiroshima and the site of the Japanese naval fleet. The instant death toll was tens of thousands. Japan had been defeated.

Since they had no radio, Yoko, her mother, and her siblings didn't know that the war had ended. But when they finally heard the news, Isoko insisted on staying away from the city until she could find out whether Tokyo's occupation by U.S. soldiers would be friendly. She brought her children to the Yasuda family home in Kamakura, where Yoko had spent her infancy. The family anxiously waited there for information about Eisuke. Isoko had had no contact with him since Hanoi fell.

At long last, in early 1946, Isoko received word from a bank official that, although Chinese forces had kept Eisuke in a prisoner-of-war camp in Hanoi for more than a year, he was all right. When Yoko heard the news, relief swept over her. She knew that everything she had gone through had been worth it, because the worst hadn't happened: Incredibly, they had all survived.

The family was reunited in Kamakura, but life would hardly return to normal. The wartime destruction made Tokyo appear ghostly and desolate, with inverted spaces where buildings should have been. "I remember how I cried at the end of the war," Yoko later wrote, "how bombed out [everything] looked when I returned from the country on the back of a truck, and what we went through daily reading about the people in Hiroshima. The ones who died of burns went quickly. The ones who died of leukemia [caused by the effects of the atomic bomb] went through a slow and agonizing death." If she had learned anything from the war, it was that "nothing was permanent. You don't want to possess anything that is dear to you because you might lose it. So I became extremely disinterested in anything material . . . I just kept everything sort of far away."

Against a backdrop of postwar chaos, adults tried to reclaim their lives by going back to work. Eisuke took yet another high-ranking position at yet another bank, although this time at least he was based in Tokyo. And adults tried to help their children reclaim *their* lives by sending them back to school, usually in overcrowded and makeshift army barracks. Yoko spent two hours every day, beginning in April 1946, commuting by train from the Yasuda home in Kamakura to Gakushūin and back. Finally the Onos moved to a house in a fashionable neighborhood closer to Tokyo's center. Yoko, now thirteen, felt guilty that some of the children at her school were extremely thin because of their wartime suffering. She, on the other hand, was once again physically hearty and, many felt, becoming quite a beauty.

Gakushūin—so protective of its illustrious student body— was surrounded by high gates, providing a safe haven. Yoko's classmates now included Emperor Hirohito's two sons. The elder, the crown prince Akihito, was Yoko's peer. (In 1989, he would become Japan's 125th emperor.) His younger brother, Yoshi, had a special bond with Yoko. They shared stories and poems they wrote, and as they matured, he developed a crush on her.

Yoko at sixteen or seventeen. She liked receiving piano lessons from her father, a former musician, because it meant spending time with him. What she didn't like was how critical he was of her playing: "Whenever I started to play, he would say, 'No, not that way, let me show you how.'"

Isoko and Eisuke tried to pick up where they had left off before the war. Once a week, Yoko and her siblings got to eat dinner with their parents. Her new nanny stood behind her chair while she ate. If Yoko demonstrated any bad table manners, her parents would reprimand the nanny—not Yoko—for failing to teach their daughter proper etiquette. Yoko ate as carefully as she could.

Now that her life had stabilized, she resumed piano lessons with an instructor. Yoko also began receiving lessons from her father. As she played the songs he had taught her, she knew that Eisuke was reflecting back on his abandoned career as a

musician, perhaps wistfully. She dearly wanted her father to compliment her, but more often than not he told her that the way she was playing was wrong. He even measured her hands to see if they were big enough for a professional career as a pianist—could her fingers stretch for the octave? "I would fall asleep at night in terror that my hands were too small to meet my father's expectations," she said.

Eisuke decided that her hands were indeed too small for a career as a pianist. He called her into his study, where he was smoking his pipe in his leather chair. He told her that she wasn't good enough and should just give up playing.

His words stung Yoko, but becoming a pianist had been Eisuke's dream for her, not her dream for herself, and she sure wouldn't miss all the practicing. She told him what had been on her mind: She wanted to be a composer.

There was silence at first. Then Eisuke tried to talk her out of it—wouldn't she much rather be a singer? Being a composer, he felt, was no job for a woman; otherwise, wouldn't there be some female composers out there to hold up as examples? He reminded his daughter that Bach, Beethoven, and Brahms—his favorite composers—were all men. Eisuke had Yoko begin taking voice lessons so that she could sing German classical songs known as lieder. This, he figured, would satisfy her love of music.

Although he didn't support her the way she hoped, Yoko was thankful that Eisuke took her goals seriously enough to talk with her about them. "In those days, the fact that a father would discuss a daughter's career was already considered quite unusual," she said later. "Daughters were brought up to go to finishing schools and hoped to get married before people started to raise their eyebrows. I am still thankful that my father cared at all about my career." As thankful as Yoko was, she still longed to be truly accepted by him. It just didn't seem possible.

She also yearned to be accepted by her mother, but she and Isoko found themselves in power struggles over Yoko's independent ideas. Yoko resented the fact that her mother, like other upper-class parents, forbade her to visit the coffee shops that were popping up all over Tokyo as the city rebounded from the war. Why, Isoko wondered, would Yoko want to fraternize with young people of a lower social class? Why, Yoko wondered, did her mother treat her like a fragile little doll?

Although Isoko didn't understand her elder daughter, she let Yoko know that she admired her desire to learn and be challenged. Isoko told Yoko that even a woman, if she were sufficiently bright, could have a career in politics or public service—a forward-thinking attitude in the 1940s.

But no matter how encouraging Isoko was about her daughter's potential—and when Yoko gave some of Isoko's friends English lessons, Isoko's pride was unmistakable—Yoko didn't completely trust her mother's or, for that matter, her father's praise. "What happened was that I began to feel they didn't love me for what I was, so much as they loved me for just being an Ono."

YOKO WAS OLDER than her classmates because she had fallen behind in her studies during the war, and this, coupled with her intelligence, helped her shine at Gakushūin. She was an advanced reader of both Japanese and English, and her Western-style outspokenness won her many friends. She became active in drama, joining the school's club, and by high school she was writing, directing, and starring in her own plays. Her friends were impressed when, instead of writing a straightforward account of a class outing, as the students had been instructed to do, Yoko dashed off a short novel about it.

But Yoko's writing wasn't encouraged by her teachers: They considered it too unconventional and hard to categorize. Still, Yoko thought that someday she might like to become not just a composer but also a writer.

The aftermath of the war brought a highly charged atmosphere bursting with ideas about democracy, freedom, and pacifism. In Tokyo and other cities around the world, an artistic rebellion was taking place that was considered *avant-garde*—a French term for ahead-of-their-time ideas in the worlds of art, theater, film, literature, and music. Yoko came of age during this period. Although her protective parents wouldn't allow her to associate with Tokyo's artistic rebels, creativity became a bigger and bigger outlet for her ongoing feelings of isolation and loneliness, which no number of friends could banish. The constant reassurance of her imagination also relieved her memories of the devastation that had surrounded her during the war. She filled notebooks with her thoughts and ideas.

When she was nineteen, Yoko came up with the optimistic *Seven Little Stories*, which actually read more like poems than like stories. "Reincarnation," the third story in the set, reads, "Mirror becomes a razor when it's broken. / A stick becomes a flute when it's loved." She was saying that seemingly useless things can have value if only we look at them in a new way. She wanted to share this idea with the shaken world, like a burst of good news.

When it was time to graduate from Gakushūin, Yoko was ready to move on. An autobiographical poem she later wrote called "Biography" summed up the restlessness that marked her youth. A section of it reads,

born: Bird Year
early childhood: collected skys
adolescence: collected sea-weeds
late adolescence: gave birth to a
      grapefruit, collected snails,
      clouds, garbage cans etc.
      Have graduated many schools
      specializing in these subjects.

But what was she going to do with her life? Yoko had begun taking opera lessons, and she considered attending the Tokyo Music School. This was seen as a suitable choice for a respectable young woman, who, unlike a young man, would never be expected to support a family.

As far as her parents were concerned, music school would be a way for her to bide her time until the right man—if not a prince, then an ambassador or someone similar—came along. There was no lack of interest. Plenty of boys from families the Onos approved of had feelings for Yoko. Prince Yoshi's crush on Yoko even inspired the Japanese press to dub Yoko his first love. But these young men just didn't interest her.

The truth was, neither did the Tokyo Music School. Yoko didn't want to sing other people's songs: She wanted to write her own. She had a new plan, but she wanted to secure her father's blessing before she went ahead with it. Dreading his disapproval, Yoko sent him a telegram in New York, where he now had a prestigious job working for the Manhattan branch of the Bank of Tokyo. She asked him if he would support her decision to enroll in Gakushūin University's philosophy course as its first female student. Eisuke expressed regret at her decision, but he gave her his blessing anyway: Yoko's intellect was something that he had never doubted.

At Gakushūin University, Yoko was dropped headlong into some intense coursework. She studied the basic philosophical *isms*—Marxism, existentialism, pacifism—and read a dizzying amount of work by great thinkers, including the Russian novelist Fyodor Dostoyevsky and the French philosopher Jean-Paul Sartre. It was impossible for Yoko and her classmates to talk about philosophy without reflecting on recent events: Wounds from the war were still raw. She impressed her teachers and peers with her intelligence, seriousness, and apparent lack of self-consciousness about being a lone woman studying what was regarded as a man's subject.

Being a bookworm, Yoko loved all the reading. But in 1953 she dropped out after only two semesters. She had become bored with academic teaching, which to her seemed rigid. But that didn't mean she had a new direction. Feeling that she might drift away, and suddenly without a compelling reason to stay in Tokyo, Yoko gave in to her parents and agreed to join them and her siblings, all now living in the upscale suburb of Scarsdale, just outside New York City.

New York was a hotbed of artistic activity and would soon provide Yoko with the sustenance she needed. Ultimately, she would reinvent herself there. For now, she continued the process of self-discovery that had been going on for some time. She was painfully aware of feeling like an outsider and being alienated from the values and traditions of her family. But Yoko was also beginning to realize that being an outsider wasn't necessarily a bad thing. ▪

Norman Seaman presents works by

YOKO ONO

A GRAPEFRUIT IN THE World of PARK

A PIECE for Strawberries AND Violin

AOS — David TUDOR

ELECTRONIC TECHNICAL ASSISTANT
RICHARD MAXFIELD

LIGHTING TECHNICAL ASSISTANT
DONALD KELLY

NOV. FRI. 6 P.M.

CARNEGIE RECITAL HALL

154 W. 57 ST.

TICKETS $1.50 AT CARNEGIE box office

2

112 CHAMBERS STREET

(1953–1962)

 Unless I rebelled . . . I wouldn't have survived. "

—YOKO ONO, 1997

At her parents' house in Scarsdale in the summer of 1953, Yoko became fascinated with the sound of birds singing in the morning outside her window. One day she decided to try to translate these sounds into musical notes that she could put on staff paper, as she had tried to do as a child in school at Jiyu Gakuen. Eventually she reached a conclusion: It was impossible. "The musical notes were too limited to express such a beautiful music that the bird was creating," Yoko explained later. But she wanted to get the birds' sound on paper somehow. So she put words, not notes, on the staff paper. She called it *Secret Piece*. It read,

> Decide on one note that you want to play.
> Play it with the following accompaniment:
> The woods from 5 a.m. to 8 a.m.
> in summer.

Yoko found that she enjoyed writing sentences that read like a poem but also like simple directions not necessarily meant to be followed. She had been told what to do all her life; with her instruction-like poems, she could give the orders and push the boundaries of the imagination. Her poems were about everyday things that she wanted to transform into magical, otherworldly objects. Yoko thought that with a little imagination, she could transform anything.

Meanwhile, Yoko longed to show her schoolmates in Japan the gorgeous American skies and the American customs—especially public displays of affection and emotion, and the lack of formality between children and their parents. Unfamiliar as it was, this extroverted behavior appealed to Yoko. It was the way she had never been allowed to act.

SECRET PIECE

Decide on one note that you want to play.
Play it with the following accompaniment:

The woods from 5 a.m. to 8 a.m.
in summer.

8ᵛ ... with the accompaniment of the birds singing at dawn

1953 summer

In the fall, Yoko began attending Sarah Lawrence College. The prestigious liberal-arts school was located in Bronxville, New York, not far from her parents' house and about a half-hour train ride from Manhattan. Sarah Lawrence offered small classes, didn't grade its students, and encouraged them to learn at their own pace. Yoko was free to study what she wanted: musical composition and literature.

Her application to the school had been accompanied by a rave recommendation from a Gakushūin teacher: Yoko would

Yoko wrote *Secret Piece* when she was twenty years old and at a crossroads in her life. Later, she would call this kind of poemlike writing an "instruction."

be "a bridge between the United States and Japan." That *sounded* good, but no matter how much Yoko accomplished there academically or creatively, and no matter how American her clothing and hairstyle, she was still considered a foreigner who just didn't fit in.

At Sarah Lawrence—which then enrolled only women, the vast majority of whom were white—Yoko stood out physically, because she was Asian, and socially, because she was quiet. Because of this, her classmates thought she was a bit peculiar. They couldn't believe that she hadn't so much as held hands with a boy, despite her many suitors at Gakushūin. But Yoko also stood out as a highly intelligent young woman with an original mind. The writer Erica Abeel, who was Yoko's room-mate at Sarah Lawrence, recalled, "My strongest visual memory of her is perching in the apple tree right on the front lawn—the great lawn in front of the main building. And she'd be up there writing haiku . . . Everyone knew her for that."

Sometimes what Yoko produced with her pen wasn't even as long as a haiku. During her lonely first semester at college, she was moved to write the stark but pleading *Smell Piece*. It read, "Send the smell of the moon." This simple line showed how she wanted to experience the universe with all of her senses.

Having few friends, Yoko spent most of her time alone. Up in the apple tree, tucked away in her dorm room, or hunkered down in the library, she produced poetry, music, and art. To those who read, heard, or saw it, her work seemed unusually sophisticated for someone only twenty years old. While her writing professors were more than impressed with her work, many found it difficult to categorize, just as Yoko's teachers at Gakushūin had. Perhaps unknowingly, Yoko's professors made her feel that there was something wrong with her.

"Whenever I wrote a poem, they said it was too long, it was like a short story; a novel was like a short story and a short story was like a poem," she said. "I felt that I was like a misfit in every medium."

Still, she continued to create her idiosyncratic work, harboring a hope that others would see what she saw in it: "I was always writing, I was sending things to the *New Yorker* and places like that and I'd get a polite refusal." She felt somewhat vindicated when one of her pieces, "A Grapefruit in the World of Park," was accepted by the *Campus*, the college newspaper, and published in the fall of 1955. In Yoko's dreamlike story, which takes place in an urban park, a grapefruit is left on a table and discovered by children who decide to eat it just because the wastebasket is too full to contain it. Peeled and consumed, the grapefruit transforms from a "greenish yellow thing, with little wrinkles around it" into a juicy, fresh fruit.

Alone, vulnerable, and with more beneath the surface than meets the eye, the grapefruit in the story shared many qualities with the author. Yoko's identification with the grapefruit had its roots in her first taste of the sweet yet sour fruit on one of her childhood visits to the United States. She was beginning to see it as a symbol of the alienation she had experienced shuttling between the East and the West, never feeling that she belonged anywhere.

At around the time "A Grapefruit in the World of Park" was published, Yoko wrote *Lighting Piece*: "Light a match and watch till it goes out." Simply lighting a match and watching the flame go out had become a private ritual that helped calm her nerves. It made her think about the fleeting nature of life—even the life of a match. She wondered if the action would have the same grounding effect on others. "I thought that there might be some people who needed something more than painting, poetry, and music," she said. Occasionally Yoko would perform *Lighting Piece* for a few of her college friends. She hoped for a glint of understanding from them, but at best their responses amounted to a tactful version of "So what?"

By the time she was a junior at Sarah Lawrence, Yoko, feeling hopelessly out of place, had practically stopped attending classes. Instead, she spent most of her time in the college's music library. She was fed up with classical music, and she would listen over and over again to any innovative work she could find. Yoko would also take the train to Manhattan and visit the library at Juilliard, the esteemed performing arts school, where she would pore over its musical scores, hoping to find what she wasn't finding elsewhere.

One day Yoko confided in her composition teacher her frustration at not being able to translate the sound of birds singing into musical notation. He had a tip for her: Why didn't she try to study with John Cage and some of the other New York composers who were exploring new, unconventional ideas about music? The truth was, Yoko was leery of studying with anybody. After years of taking lessons upon lessons, she had come to see instructors as people intent on forcing her to strive for a single fixed goal, almost like painting by numbers. Still, her interest in these New York artists was piqued.

She began riding the train into the city whenever she had the opportunity. There she explored experimental art and music by seeking out edgy galleries and attending concerts considered underground, or operating outside the mainstream. New York's Greenwich Village had become the center of a subculture of freethinkers known as the beat generation, which was loosely made up of writers (such as Allen Ginsberg

and Jack Kerouac), painters, and musicians. The beats—or beatniks, as they were called—were tired of what they considered the country's postwar complacency. Instead, they wanted to wake up—and shake up—the typical white, middle-class American family.

Yoko took on the beat look by wearing little makeup, dressing in simple all-black outfits, and growing her hair long—"It was such an improper thing to do, to grow your hair," she said later with some pride. As she spent more and more time in Manhattan, Yoko found herself less and less interested in school. Despite her parents' and teachers' protestations, she dropped out of Sarah Lawrence after her junior year. She was "sick and tired of that middle-class scene"—the value system adopted by her parents. Yoko saw them as creative people who had given up their artistic aspirations in order to uphold the family image of respectability, which to her meant conformity. She was clear that she didn't want what had happened to her father, whose dream of being a musician had died, to happen to her.

Yoko was influenced by the beats, a group of artists and writers who wanted to wake up and shake up the older generation—squares, in the language of the day. Gathered at a restaurant in New York in the mid-1950s are (*left to right*) artist Larry Rivers, writer Jack Kerouac, poet Gregory Corso (*back of head to camera*), musician David Amram, and poet Allen Ginsberg, who would become Yoko's friend.

She may not have shared her parents' values, but Yoko was once again living under their roof.

ONE NIGHT AT a party in the city attended by many musicians, Yoko met Toshi Ichiyanagi, a prodigy with a scholarship to the Juilliard School. Toshi, who had a disarmingly gentle manner, was a Japanese pianist and composer with an interest in electronic music and the avant-garde. The two shared not only a similar cultural heritage but also an almost palpable artistic drive. Yoko admired Toshi's talent and appreciated that he wanted to break away from the traditional musicianship usually taught at conservatories like Juilliard. She was also intrigued by the promise of freedom that his life as an artist would afford him.

Yoko and Toshi began a romance—it was Yoko's first serious one. Her parents immediately disapproved. Toshi didn't have much money or come from a prominent family, and they felt that he would bring dishonor to the Yasuda-Ono clan. Isoko and Eisuke—who had, they seemed to have conveniently forgotten, married for love—warned their daughter that if she didn't end the romance, they would disown her. Yoko reminded them that Eisuke had been considered unworthy of marrying Isoko because he was a musician from a lower social class, but her argument didn't change their minds. They pointed out that Eisuke had given up his musical career in part for Isoko— would Toshi do the same for Yoko?

It was among her parents' worst fears that their pedigreed and well-bred daughter would live the life of a starving artist, but that's exactly what she did. Yoko eloped with Toshi in 1956 and moved with him into an apartment at 426 Amsterdam Avenue, in uptown Manhattan. Isoko and Eisuke couldn't turn their hearts completely to stone, however, so they rented a large ballroom for the couple's wedding reception. But to protest her daughter's bohemian lifestyle, Isoko stopped sending her money to live on.

Marriage wasn't a cure for her loneliness, but it did provide Yoko with companionship, and the buzz of activity in the city was often comforting. She soaked up the sensations that came with her new life, including the sounds of trucks rattling down the street and the smells outside her window: "I was living next to a meat market and I felt as if I had a house with a delicatessen in it." New York worked its way into her writing at the time, including *Central Park Pond Piece*, which reflected her coming to terms with cutting ties with her family: "Go to the middle of the Central Park / Pond and drop all your jewelry." Yoko made the same statement when she would wash her face and, instead of using a towel, pointedly dry it on a delicate cocktail dress. In her own unique way she was expressing what she thought of stuffy middle-class values.

Through Toshi, Yoko was introduced to a group of adventurous artists working in different media: music, performance, dance, filmmaking, painting, sculpture, and writing, and sometimes more than one at a time. She met cutting-edge New York art-world luminaries, including John Cage, the minimalist composer her composition teacher at Sarah Lawrence had told her about. Yoko found the work of these artists compelling, but she also knew that it wasn't quite the kind of art she wanted to create.

To make ends meet, Toshi got sporadic work in his field, playing concerts and copying musical scores. Yoko brought in money on different occasions as a typist, a translator, and a teacher of Japanese folk art. She and Toshi were hired by

New York's Japan Society, an organization focused on Japanese culture, to perform in programs for various groups—both locally and at colleges that included Harvard University. Yoko recited traditional Japanese poems and demonstrated Japanese calligraphy, origami techniques, flower arranging, and tea ceremonies. At times she felt like nothing more than a curiosity, but at least she didn't have to grovel to her parents for rent money.

Working odd jobs left the couple financially insecure, but this lifestyle granted Yoko the time she needed to immerse herself in her art. She began creating calligraphic abstract paintings with sumi ink, which is traditionally used for calligraphy in Japan. As her visual art, writing, and performances (the term *performance art* hadn't yet been coined) like *Lighting Piece* were evolving, Yoko found herself bombarded with so many creative ideas that at times she had to withdraw into herself. "I knew then that I was into something special and that was the cause of my loneliness," she said. "The thought of being able to do something, the thought that I may be able to leave a mark on the world excited me tremendously, but can you imagine having all those ideas and nowhere to go with them, nowhere to present them?" She was at once frustrated by not having an outlet and not quite sure what others would think of her work if and when she discovered one.

In the fall of 1960, Yoko found herself fantasizing about having a space where she could put on her own exhibitions and performances as well as those of other avant garde artists. One brittle October day, while wandering around a gritty industrial area in downtown Manhattan's Lower West Side, now known as Tribeca, she saw a sign advertising a loft for rent on the top floor of a five-floor walk-up at 112 Chambers Street, two blocks from the Hudson River. She inquired about the space and received a tour. The stairs leading up to the loft seemed endless, but the trek was worth it.

The long rectangular space was nearly two thousand square feet—big enough for two good-size swimming pools. Its only windows were at the back and front, and the ceiling wasn't high, but Yoko felt that it would be a terrific place for artists to share their work and watch one another perform. And the space had another redeeming feature besides its size: a skylight, which couldn't help but hold special meaning for Yoko, who had relied on the sky for reassurance during the war.

Although the rumble of heavy traffic on Chambers Street never let up and the entire building shook whenever the Eighth Avenue subway raced beneath the street, Yoko was sold. "The night after I looked at that space, I felt my whole fate was sealed . . . I was thinking, 'I *have* to get that place.'"

Yoko at her Chambers Street loft with her husband, Toshi Ichiyanagi (at the piano), and composer Toshiro Mayuzumi. Yoko had asked some friends to paint the loft in exchange for using it as a performance space. "Everyone was lazy and didn't get around to painting it white," she said later, "but I got used to the gray."

There was fierce competition for the loft, which did not even have hot running water, but Yoko got it—for $50.50 a month. Once she and Toshi moved in, she was not disappointed by her somewhat primitive living situation. "All the windows were smoked glass so that you couldn't really see outside, but there was the skylight, and when you were in the loft you almost felt more connected to the sky than to the city outside . . . It was great. I didn't have chairs or beds, and so people downstairs gave me orange crates and I put all the crates together to make a large table, crates for the chairs, and at night I just collected them and made a bed out of them."

Yoko wasn't the only one who saw the loft's potential. Shortly after she and Toshi moved in, a friend approached them about opening their home to a group of artists who were interested in presenting their work. Plans got under way to turn the loft into a center for concerts and artistic events, also known as happenings, performed by and for the New York experimental-arts community. But Yoko was having a problem with some of the artists, most of whom were male. Several of them referred to her as the "owner" of the loft rather than as an artist in her own right.

In fact, these artists didn't initially include her in their plans. "There was no mention that I should have a concert there," Yoko said. "Many people thought that I was a very rich girl who was just 'playing avant-garde.' And some others thought that I was a mistress of some very rich man, which wasn't true either . . . And meanwhile I was just surviving by teaching Japanese folk art." She finally had it out with one of the men. "I had to say, 'I know you are a very talented artist. All you have to do is to reciprocate that and just realize that I am also a talented artist.'"

Yoko's nerves were jangling the night of the first Chambers Street concert. To heat the room she had to use an old gas stove that had a fan. She and Toshi couldn't afford to pay their electric bill and hadn't yet figured out how to get electricity from the outlet in the hallway. "But it was beautiful; we did it under candlelight," Yoko recalled.

Not only did people come to the loft concerts, known as the Chambers Street series and organized principally by Yoko and the avant-garde musician La Monte Young, but she helped start a trend. Other artists began to flock to the area, and also to an adjacent neighborhood that had been a fabric district but in the late 1960s would become known as Soho, which evolved into what would be for decades the heart of the New York art world. In the early 1960s, lofts in Tribeca and Soho were cheap, providing artists with wide-open spaces in which to live and create.

To advertise the Chambers Street series, Yoko, Toshi, and their friends would put up flyers in coffee houses and other neighborhood shops, but word of mouth usually did the trick. Even in the dead of winter, the loft concerts became the place to be, attracting John Cage, the composer Philip Glass, the choreographer Merce Cunningham, the painters Robert Rauschenberg and Jasper Johns, and the art patron Peggy Guggenheim, who had been the famous abstract expressionist Jackson Pollock's art dealer.

Also in attendance at Chambers Street were, to Yoko's delight, Peggy Guggenheim's ex-husband Max Ernst, the German painter; and Marcel Duchamp, the French artist. Both men had been figureheads of an early twentieth century art movement known as Dada. Dada had blossomed during

World War I as a protest against what the artists felt were the greed and materialism that had caused the conflict. It was also a reaction to pretentious (and pretentious-sounding) art movements that took themselves too seriously, which explained Dada's nonsensical name. In what was for many the ultimate Dada gesture, in 1917 Duchamp submitted to an art show a piece he called *Fountain*: a men's urinal that he had mysteriously signed "R. Mutt," as an artist would sign his or her own creation. The art world was equal parts shocked and amused.

Beate Sirota Gordon, then the performing-arts director of the Japan Society, climbed the well-worn stairs leading up to the loft one night. "The large room was bare except for a refrigerator, some wooden beer barrels that served as seats, and a handful of spectators, among them a reporter," she wrote. That evening Yoko was presenting one of her first performances, which she called *Kitchen Piece*. Its text read,

Hang a canvas on a wall.
Throw all the leftovers you have
in the kitchen that day on the
canvas.
You may prepare special food for
the piece.

"Yoko ran to the refrigerator, took out some eggs, ran to a wall covered with a huge piece of white paper, and hurled eggs onto the paper," Gordon continued. "Then she ran back and got some Jell-O, which she threw at the wall. Then she splattered some sumi ink on the paper and used her hands as paintbrushes. When the painting was completed, she took a match and set fire to the paper . . . Luckily, John Cage had warned Yoko to put a fire retardant on the paper, so it burned slowly."

At another performance, called *Pea Piece*, whose text read, "Carry a bag of peas. / Leave a pea wherever you go," Yoko tossed peas at her audience while whirling her long black hair in a circle, which to her was a kind of musical accompaniment. Most members of her audience had no idea that throwing peas out of the house is an old, annual Japanese ritual meant to expunge the devil and bring good luck. After the performance, one of Yoko's friends complained that it was too theatrical, but Yoko didn't mind: "If I throw a pea around, most people would think it was crazy or insane, but among our friends it was something serious to criticize."

Unfortunately, Yoko's personal life didn't hold the promise of her creative life. Her relationship with Toshi had begun to shift, and the couple separated in early 1961. Although she cared deeply about him, Yoko was having a tough time with the adoration that he was receiving from the art world. She was working just as intensely on her art as he was on his, and yet "it was hard to make people understand that I was an artist too." Her frustration led her to seek validation elsewhere: "I was having affairs and things like that to compensate, so our relationship deteriorated." She felt so guilty about betraying Toshi, whose sweet nature allowed him to forgive her every indiscretion, that she finally encouraged him to go back to Japan, where she couldn't continue to hurt him.

After Toshi returned to Tokyo that summer, his career as a composer really took off. He and Yoko still had strong feelings for each other and weren't ready to call it quits, so they stayed in touch.

ON HAND AT some of the Chambers Street series events was a scholarly eccentric named George Maciunas, who was living nearby when he learned of the loft events from La Monte Young. He became so inspired by the loft concerts that he opened AG Gallery, uptown at 925 Madison Avenue, so that he could present his own boundary-flouting exhibitions and events. The initials *AG* came from the first names of George and his partner, Almus Salcius, but some believed that *AG* stood for *avant-garde*.

Yoko first met the charismatic impresario when the loft events were at the peak of their popularity. "Two hundred people were coming," she said. "Then I was told that everybody was going to perform at a gallery on Madison Avenue instead. I was a bit hurt; I asked who was doing it. 'George Maciunas, he was at your concert the other day, don't you remember?' . . . He stole my idea, I thought . . . [but] then I got a call from George asking if I would do a one-woman show in his gallery. That was the start of a great friendship, but I didn't know it yet."

Maciunas scheduled Yoko's first visual-art show for July 1961. For the show's title, she decided on *Paintings and Drawings by Yoko Ono*—a deliberately misleading name, as there was not a single painting or drawing in the traditional sense on view. She was still intent on trying to establish a new way to think about art, and she took that leap with what she called her instruction paintings.

Yoko had no interest in just making a conventional painting and hanging it on the wall. She thought that once a traditional painting was finished, it was dead. She wanted her work to be ongoing, spontaneous, and alive. One way to keep it alive was for it to be unfinished. For the AG Gallery show, she wrote down her ideas on paper, as she had with *Secret Piece, Smell*

Piece, *Lighting Piece*, *Central Park Pond Piece*, *Kitchen Piece*, *Pea Piece*, and many others. These step-by-step suggestions, which read like instructions, were posted alongside canvases that the viewer was asked to either physically change in some way or just imagine changing.

Painting for the Wind consisted of a bag of seeds hanging in front of a canvas. The instruction read, "Cut a hole in a bag filled with seeds / of any kind and place the bag where / there is wind." (Yoko had made a hole in the canvas so that the wind could blow through it.) But viewers could also just imagine cutting a hole in the bag and watching the seeds scatter in the wind. It was up to them to decide which instruction paintings were meant to spur them to actually do something and which were only meant to spur their imaginations.

It was up to viewers to decide if they should literally follow Yoko's instructions or just imagine doing so.

PAINTING FOR THE WIND

Cut a hole in a bag filled with seeds of any kind and place the bag where there is wind.

1961 summer

Most of the instruction paintings were hung on the gallery's brick walls, but not *Painting to Be Stepped On*, which read, "Leave a piece of canvas or finished / painting on the floor or in the street." (Yoko had already exhibited *Painting to Be Stepped On* at the Chambers Street series on a night when Marcel Duchamp was in attendance. She had been crushed that he hadn't noticed it, much less stepped on it.) For most viewers, the floor was the last place on earth they'd expect to find a painting, which was typically framed to protect it and then hung with care and reverence on a wall. At Yoko's show, visitors were free to step all over an oddly shaped fragment of canvas—or, if they weren't comfortable doing that, they could just imagine stepping on it. She loved the idea that people could finish a work of art just by using their minds. When they did so, Yoko felt, they became artists. Not only that, but because everyone, no matter what age, has an imagination, she was starting to think of all people as artists and of art as not just for museums and galleries but flowing into everyday life.

Paintings and Drawings by Yoko Ono was sparsely attended, and AG Gallery had to close when the show ended because Maciunas and his partner couldn't wrangle the funds to keep it going. But Yoko did receive a short write-up in the respected *ARTnews* magazine, and she was hopeful that she had gotten through to at least some of those who had seen her work.

After about a year of hosting the Chambers Street series, Yoko stopped. She just didn't find it exciting anymore. But she was still full of inspiration and determined to make a name for herself in New York's avant-garde art world, and not only with her instruction paintings. She had performed several times outside of the Chambers Street series, and on November 24, 1961, she debuted some new work at New York's Carnegie Recital

COMPOSER—Yoko Ono
will have a program of
her works performed in
concert Friday evening.

Hall, located in midtown Manhattan next door to the legendary and larger Carnegie Hall. Although the event, *Works by Yoko Ono*, was billed as a solo performance, she enlisted the help of some friends.

The lights were dimmed while performers read newspapers in various languages, using flashlights or match flames to see. A tape recorder played speeches in different languages by public figures, including Japan's Emperor Hirohito. A woman stuck her hands and legs through an opening in the stage's

One of the pieces Yoko produced for *Works by Yoko Ono* was a tribute to David Tudor, an avant-garde musician she and Toshi had gotten to know. Yoko considered the piece an opera of "blue chaos," and she titled her piece *AOS—To David Tudor* in homage ("ao" is Japanese for "blue," and "os" is from the English word "chaos").

curtain. On several occasions during the evening, a toilet could be heard flushing. At one point two men with empty cans and bottles at their feet were wrapped back-to-back with gauze, and Yoko instructed them to move from one end of the stage to the other while trying not to make a sound. Contact microphones had been attached to them so that subtle bodily noises like their breathing and gestures could be picked up. The two figures appeared both tragic and comic as they tried to move away from each other without really going anywhere.

The audience had never seen or heard anything like it. "There are unknown areas of sound and experience that people can't really mention in words," Yoko said, explaining the piece. "Like the stuttering in your mind. I was interested not in the noise you make but the noise that happens when you try not to make it, just that tension going back and forth." By keeping the room dark, she was hoping to capture "the sound of fear and of darkness, like a child's fear that someone is behind him, but he can't speak and communicate this." For this reason Yoko had a male friend stand at the back of the audience throughout the performance.

While she sensed that this was groundbreaking work, it was also draining, and the show received negative reviews. Yoko began to wonder if her work might be better received in another environment, and she knew that Tokyo had a thriving art scene. Long conflicted about her Japanese American identity, she wanted to try to reconnect with her homeland. (Isoko and Eisuke, with whom she continued to have a chilly relationship, were still in Scarsdale.) Plus, relocating to Tokyo would give her and Toshi a chance to see if anything was left of their marriage.

So in March 1962 Yoko moved back to Tokyo, settling in an

empty studio apartment owned by her parents in a high-rise building. She was surprised and even somewhat amused to find that the city had become so Americanized—architecturally, fashionwise, attitudewise—in the near decade that she had been away.

Upon arriving in Japan, Yoko wasted no time romantically (Toshi moved in with her) or artistically: Toshi had arranged for her to have a show at Tokyo's Sogetsu Art Center, a venue for avant-garde art and performance. On May 24 she presented *Works of Yoko Ono*, which included instructions, events, and what she called touch poems. One touch poem took the form of a small book whose wordless pages exhibited human hair.

The performances that Yoko presented at Sogetsu included *Question Piece*, which consisted of two people asking each other questions but providing no answers. For *The Pulse*, performers sat doing Yoko's handwritten math problems at a table with a microphone on it, accompanied by the sounds of, among other things, birds singing. Yoko also presented *Audience Piece*, in which she instructed performers—she was one— to stand on the stage and stare at the audience. Nearly two dozen people stood in line at the edge of the stage, arms by their sides or in their pockets, eyes on their perplexed onlookers. Hours later they were sitting or reclining on the stage, their focus no less intense on the audience, which by then had significantly dwindled. Sogetsu's administration finally shut down the event after one in the morning.

By making the audience members the ones who were being watched for a change, Yoko got them to bring their own ideas and even their anxieties to the art experience. A lot of artists didn't care what their audiences thought, but she had high expectations of hers.

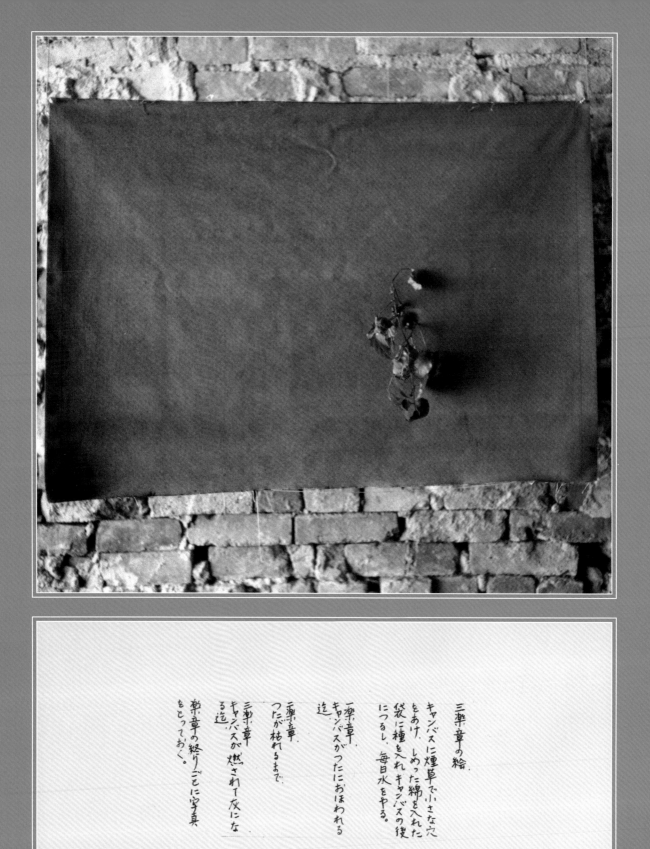

三楽章の絵.

キャンバスに煙草で小さな穴
をあけ、しめった綿を入れた
袋に種を入れ、キャンバスの後
につるし、毎日水をやる。

一楽章.
キャンバスがつたにおほわれる
迄.

二楽章.
つたが枯れるまで.

三楽章.
キャンバスが燃されて灰にな
る迄.

楽章の終りごとに写真
をとっておく.

At the AG Gallery show the previous year, Yoko's instruction paintings had made plain her belief that the idea behind a painting is more important than the painting itself. At the Sogetsu exhibition, she went even further. This time around, instead of providing canvases and other tangible props that the viewer could physically handle, she literally exhibited ideas themselves, in written form, on the wall. Now she was saying that ideas *themselves* can be art.

While Yoko was brave to present daring art in a country that barely recognized women as artists, the negative reviews that her work received hurt her, as they would any artist, and led to rejection by her peers. "At dinners some would make a point of not speaking to me or not sitting near me," she said. But a lot of the criticism leveled at her was not about her art. Yoko recalled one reviewer writing about "women wearing pants coming back from abroad who think they know something."

But Yoko couldn't stop making art her way just because some people didn't like it. About the Sogetsu show she later wrote, "Forget the disappointment caused by people's reaction—or nonreaction. Coming up with the idea, preparing for the show, and finally exhibiting [the ideas] as paintings: All that was terribly exciting. It was like a love affair." ▪

TOP Yoko's *Painting in Three Stanzas* (canvas version), from the summer of 1961. The corresponding instruction reads,

> Let a vine grow.
> Water every day.
> The first stanza—till the vine spreads.
> The second stanza—till the vine withers.
> The third stanza—till the vine dies.

BOTTOM *Painting in Three Stanzas* (text version), from 1962. Yoko believed that words, and even ideas themselves, could be art. She wanted viewers to ask: What makes something a painting? What makes something *not* a painting?

3

FLYING

(1962–1966)

" *My events are mostly spent in wonderment* "

—YOKO ONO, 1966

PAGE 50 Yoko performs *Chair Piece (Chair Ascension)* at Tokyo's Sogetsu Art Center in 1962. Later her friend the writer Kate Millett said, "Yoko was utterly fearless in the face of Japan's tedious Victorian conventions . . . She was doing a daring art form in a country that hardly permitted women to participate in the art world at all."

Not only was Yoko's work not appreciated, but she was also beginning to feel limited by the avant-garde scene and overshadowed by the men in her life, including John Cage, who, with Yoko and Toshi's help, had come to Japan to perform his work. Toshi was becoming increasingly celebrated in the experimental-music world, and John Cage was becoming internationally famous.

All the years of not fitting in, being misunderstood, and feeling that she was on the cusp of something important artistically that no one else recognized came to a head in Tokyo. Yoko felt depleted. Toshi was worried about her, and yet his mind was also on his work. "There was much emotional turmoil in my personal life . . . and I felt depressed," Yoko wrote later. She knew that she needed help managing her pain, so she decided to spend some time in a mental health clinic. "At that point, being taken care of in any form seemed a glorious option," she wrote. "I grabbed the opportunity."

When she returned to the high-rise apartment and life with the supremely busy and preoccupied Toshi a few weeks later, Yoko couldn't get over how much a New Yorker named Tony Cox, who had heard about her work and visited her in the clinic, had done for her confidence. She would often meet him at a café, where they would talk endlessly, reminiscing about New York—its neighborhoods, its coffee shops—which she missed terribly. The two became romantically involved. Once Yoko had secured a divorce from Toshi, whom she loved as a dear friend but, she had come to realize, no more than that, she and Tony got married.

If Yoko's parents had been upset by their daughter's marriage to Toshi, they were appalled by the news that she had divorced him and was now married to someone who wasn't

Yoko performs John Cage's *Music Walk* at Sogetsu Art Center in 1962, with composers (*left to right*) John Cage, David Tudor, and Toshiro Mayuzumi. To present *Music Walk* a participant may play a piano, turn on a radio, or use his or her voice to create sounds. For her contribution, Yoko turned her body into a musical instrument.

even Japanese. To pay the rent, the newlyweds did everything from dub Japanese film dialogue into English to teach Japanese businessmen how to speak English, as Yoko had taught her mother's friends to speak the language after the war. Before, after, and between jobs, Yoko would return to what she knew was her real work: her art.

On August 3, 1963, Yoko gave birth to a baby girl she and Tony named Kyoko. The child hadn't been planned, but Yoko was taken by the adorable little tot, and of course she wanted her daughter to have every happiness. Still, she was worried about what she'd taken on. Most new parents wonder how they will balance their work with meeting their child's needs, but the work that Yoko had chosen was especially consuming. "I was still struggling to get my own space in the world," she said. "I felt that if I didn't have room for myself, how could I give room to another human being?"

Tony, a big supporter and an increasingly shrewd promoter of Yoko's work, was happy to take on a major role in Kyoko's care. "That was . . . something that Yoko felt very strongly about, that if she had kids, the husband should help take care of them," Tony said later. Yoko knew one thing for sure: She wanted her child to have hands-on parents, because Isoko and Eisuke's hands-off approach had made her feel as though she had barely existed. Then again, hands-off parenting wasn't a choice for her and Tony: They could hardly afford a string of nannies like the ones who had minded Yoko.

Despite Yoko's new role as a mother and her ongoing need to, like Tony, work odd jobs to make ends meet, she remained an integral part of Tokyo's underground art scene. Before Kyoko was even a year old, Yoko brought her onstage as "an instrument—an uncontrollable instrument."

Yoko continued to help organize events and perform her own and other artists' work. Along with the electronic-art innovator Nam June Paik, a New York friend who was in Tokyo at the time, she introduced members of Japan's avant-garde to other international artists who came on the scene. She was helping to forge a coalition of creative people who shared an interest in questioning—even subverting—the status quo.

She certainly did this in the spring of 1964 with the performance piece *Fly*. In the summer of 1963 Yoko had written the instruction *Fly Piece*, which simply read, "Fly." The first performance of the instruction was to take place the following April at Tokyo's Naiqua Gallery, and the postcard she mailed out to advertise the show read, "Come prepared to fly."

The piece began when audience members were asked to come onstage and jump off a ladder, simulating flight. (The ladders were adjusted to the comfort level of each person so that he or she wouldn't get injured.) Yoko saw the idea of flying as a metaphor for freedom, and she intended the experience of jumping off the ladder as a way to help participants overcome their fears of taking emotional risks in life. She later wrote with satisfaction that "each person who attended the night flew in his/her own way."

While she was devoted to creating her unprecedented events, Yoko continued to write her poemlike instructions. Whether the instructions were to be performed or just imagined, she wanted readers to use them as a way to tap their own creativity. Expressing a wide range of thoughts, moods, fantasies, and feelings, the instructions could be funny, as in *Map Piece* ("Draw a map to get lost"); puzzling, as in *Fog Piece III* ("Send a fog to your friend"); or fanciful, as in *Cloud Piece* ("Imagine the clouds dripping. / Dig a hole in your garden to / put them in").

By now Yoko had amassed so many instructions that a book seemed like the best means of getting them to a wider audience—especially an audience that didn't tend to go to galleries or events featuring edgy young artists' work. In the summer of 1964 she self-published a book containing more than one hundred and fifty of her instructions. She printed five hundred copies of it, most in English but some in Japanese. The book had a plain white cover; Yoko couldn't afford anything fancier.

She titled her book *Grapefruit*, which harked back to "A Grapefruit in the World of Park," her story published in the Sarah Lawrence newspaper. The first copies of the book became available on July 4, 1964—a date that Yoko had chosen knowing it to be a day when Americans celebrate freedom. She predicted that the book's publication would also be freeing for her: With *Grapefruit*, she was scattering her ideas in the wind, like the seeds in her instruction *Painting for the Wind*.

Because writing the book had a therapeutic effect on her, Yoko later said that "*Grapefruit* was like a cure for myself without [my] knowing it." The first edition, which was published on July 4, 1964, had a plain white cover because Yoko couldn't afford anything fancier. She couldn't have known then that *Grapefruit* would later be reissued with different covers and in different languages.

She carried around copies of the book in an orange crate and showed them to people on the street: "I sold a few, but mostly I gave them away."

Grapefruit was considered little more than a poetic novelty and was hardly noticed by critics or the public. But the book's lack of critical or popular attention at that time didn't reflect its eventual significance. Yoko's instructions ended up having a powerful impact on one of the most important art developments of the 1960s: conceptual art.

Many artists were tired of the emotionally charged, paint-splattered works of Jackson Pollock and the other abstract expressionists who had been the postwar era's most popular art makers. They were tired of paint, period. Stripping down art to its bare bones, conceptual artists tried to make people think about art in a completely new way. These artists were creating work that was brainy but usually simple-looking. For *Box with the Sound of Its Own Making*, the artist Robert Morris exhibited a wooden box containing a tape recorder playing the recorded sounds—sawing and hammering, measuring and fitting—that he had created while making the object. For *Iron Curtain*, the husband-and-wife art team Christo and Jeanne-Claude blocked off a Paris side street with oil barrels; for them the resulting traffic jam, not the oil-barrel barricade, was the work of art. Conceptualists felt that creating art was mainly a thought process. It was the *idea* they cared about, not the product it became—if there even was a product.

Yoko's instructions made her one of the first artists to turn language into visual art. Her quietly trailblazing little book and her wholly original shows featuring her instruction paintings helped lay the groundwork for conceptual art. The critic David Bourdon later wrote that her approach to art "was only made acceptable when white men like [Joseph] Kosuth and [Lawrence] Weiner came in and did virtually the same things as Yoko, but made them respectable and collectible."

When *Grapefruit* came out, Yoko wasn't thinking about art movements. Besides, she had never liked the idea of being limited by a label, particularly a superserious-sounding one like "conceptual artist." Sometimes she told people that what she created was "con art." This reflected both her interest in challenging the often self-important art world and her sly sense of humor, which was increasingly showing up in her work. Whether people *recognized* it as humor was another story.

INITIALLY, YOKO THOUGHT that she would be away from New York for only a short time—after all, who could have known that not long after arriving in Japan she would meet and marry Tony, and then have a baby? Before she knew it, more than two years had gone by. Yet in all that time in Japan, she had never stopped feeling like a stranger.

Yoko and Tony Cox performing *Bag Piece* at Sogetsu Art Center in 1964. One of Yoko's inspirations for "bagism" was the children's book *The Little Prince*, by Antoine de Saint-Exupéry. In the story, a wise fox tells the prince that to understand the world we have to look beneath the surface: "One sees clearly only with the heart. Anything essential is invisible to the eyes."

Not long after *Grapefruit*'s publication, Yoko decided that she was ready to head back to New York City. She didn't have family or an apartment there, but when she thought of Manhattan, she actually felt homesick—a new sensation for someone who had never felt at home anywhere. To say good-bye to Tokyo, she presented *Yoko Ono Farewell Concert* at Sogetsu Art Center. It featured a work that had become, like her instructions, a signature piece.

Yoko had first begun performing *Bag Piece* alone in 1961, in New York, and it had evolved to enlist two performers (she was usually one). The performers got inside a large black bag, which was made out of a fabric that allowed them to see out but didn't allow the audience to see in. It was the viewer's job to come to his or her own conclusion about what was going on inside the bag. From the audience's standpoint, the performers in the writhing bag might be busy removing all their clothes (occasionally a garment would end up on the floor outside the bag) and then putting them back on. When the bag was still, it looked as though the performers might be napping. The piece

ended when the performers emerged from the bag and left the stage, taking the bag with them.

Bag Piece, like so many of Yoko's ideas, looked simple but had a complex meaning. She wanted to force viewers to consider how much they knew based on what they saw—or what they thought they saw. "The point was the outline of the bag, the movement of the bag: how much we see of a person," she said. "Inside there might be a lot going on. Or maybe nothing's going on." It was a desire not to be seen that had led to Yoko's first performance of the piece. She had felt near-incapacitating shyness when she and Toshi were living on Amsterdam Avenue in New York. "When people visited, I wanted to be in a big sort of box with little holes where nobody could see me but I could see through the holes," she said. "So, later, that developed into my *Bag Piece*, where you can be inside and see outside, but they can't see you."

After Yoko, Tony, and Kyoko flew back to New York, Yoko was warmly welcomed into an art scene that was explosive and energizing. She resumed her friendships with old pals, and she got to know Andy Warhol, the shock-haired pop-art prince. Warhol had taken familiar commercial images—a Campbell's soup can, a head shot of the Hollywood legend Marilyn Monroe—and duplicated and changed them until they'd become celebrated works of art. Yoko loved his mischievous sense of humor.

When she hooked up again with George Maciunas, he was involved with an innovative art group he had dubbed Fluxus, from the Latin word *influxus*, meaning "a flowing in." Fluxus consisted of a group of freewheeling artists who didn't just question the meaning and presentation of art, as the conceptualists did and the Dadaists had before them:

OPPOSITE An advertisement to promote Fluxus's "Do It Yourself" Dance Festival. The advertisement ran with the instruction *Do It Yourself Dance Piece.*

They tried to break down the boundaries between art and ordinary life. Maciunas wanted to leave professional artists out of the picture to help shatter the mystique surrounding art. He was committed to taking art literally off its pedestal—out of galleries and museums—and sending it into the world. This might mean an artist cheaply mass-producing something he or she had created—a booklet or a poster, or maybe a box or another small object—and circulating those multiples, showing that anyone can make art and that others besides millionaires can own it.

Staging events in established settings, like New York's Carnegie Recital Hall, or alternative spaces, like lofts, stairwells, and the street, Fluxus artists tried to reinvent art, often using humor. Among many memorable performances were Alison Knowles making a salad and Dick Higgins creating musical sounds with splashing water. Lasting from minutes to sometimes days, Fluxus performances carried a sense of absurdity, curiosity, and openness, leaving audiences thinking about things in new ways.

In forming Fluxus, Maciunas had been influenced by John Cage, who believed that all aspects of daily life, including turning on a light or walking out the door, could be art. But Maciunas had been primarily inspired by Yoko, whose ideas about art being completed in the mind and with the viewer's help were of particular interest to him. Yoko both preserved her independence and kept up close ties with Fluxus artists, often performing and collaborating with them.

While the group was attracting a lot of attention, Yoko, Tony, and Kyoko continued to live humbly. They found themselves moving from apartment to apartment in search of cheaper and cheaper rents. As usual, their day jobs were catch-as-catch-can.

do it yourself
dance piece:
SWIM IN YOUR SLEEP
GO ON SWIMMING UNTIL YOU
FIND AN ISLAND
YOKO ONO 1966

Yoko worked as an interpreter, and for a while she cooked and waited tables at a restaurant serving macrobiotic food—meals mainly made up of whole grains and vegetables. But earning money meant having less free time, and the couple wanted to maximize the hours that Yoko could spend on her art. By now Kyoko, raven-haired and diminutive like her mother, often watched Yoko work. Yoko and Tony believed that exposing their daughter to the process of art making would spur her natural-born inquisitiveness and creativity.

Sometimes Yoko felt as though her career still wasn't going anywhere, and her unhappiness made itself apparent to others. She would withdraw, and the long black drapes of hair framing her face were like curtains that kept her partly hidden from the world.

WHILE YOKO WAS busy conceiving and producing Fluxus pieces, she was also exploring yet another medium: objects. Unlike a sculpture, which an artist labors over with his or her own hands, an object—a ball, say, or a fork or an orange—is already in the world. With a nod to Marcel Duchamp and his "ready-mades," like the urinal he had famously submitted to an art show, Yoko took objects out of the context of the everyday and literally put them on display to change the way we think about them. One object she made was *Eternal Time*, which presented a clock that had a second hand but no hour or minute hand. Viewers knew that time was passing but not what time it was or how much time was going by. Yoko placed the clock on a Plexiglas stand from which she hung a stethoscope so that viewers could listen to time ticking away—or was that the sound of their heartbeats? Was there a difference?

All of Yoko's original and provocative pieces were daring in their own way. But at Carnegie Recital Hall, on March 21, 1965, as part of *New Works of Yoko Ono*, she reintroduced herself to the New York art world with her most shocking and challenging piece to date. For *Cut Piece*, which she had debuted the year before in Japan, Yoko, wearing her best black dress, sat alone onstage, her legs tucked discreetly under her. In her quiet voice, she asked members of the audience to come onstage and cut off pieces of her clothing with scissors she had placed on the floor before her.

Yoko performing *Cut Piece* in New York in 1965. The documentary filmmaker Albert Maysles, who filmed it, said about the piece, "It's a test of her courage . . . and it's also a test of the decency or indecency of others who may or may not exploit her vulnerability."

It took a few moments for the first person—a man—to find the nerve to approach the stage, but after he did, others—both male and female—followed suit. The only noises Yoko heard were the occasional cough from the audience, the footsteps of people walking on the stage, and the snipping of the scissors, which she thought of as a kind of music. Working hard to show no emotion—no easy feat, considering how nervous she was—Yoko sat there while, one by one, people cut her dress and even her bra until she was practically naked. Shreds of fabric were strewn on the floor around her, although some of the audience members took the fabric they had snipped back to their seats. Yoko decided that the piece was finished when there was almost nothing left to cut.

The people watching *Cut Piece* had to really look at themselves in order to decide if they were going to go onstage and do what Yoko had asked them to. If they went up and cut off pieces of her clothes, then they were helping to carry out the humiliating act of publicly undressing a woman. If they just sat there passively and watched other people do it, then they were permitting what was happening onstage. Even more confusing, just sitting there also meant that they weren't doing what the artist had said she wanted them to do (or *did* she really want them to?).

Cut Piece received no reviews but created a buzz in New York's avant-garde circles. Why would Yoko leave herself so open to exploitation, to harm, in front of so many strangers? Actually, she didn't see the piece this way. For her, the piece wasn't about having something taken from her (her clothes, her respect) but about giving—and giving everything she had.

One day, when she was missing the sky because the smoked glass of her apartment windows made it impossible to see clearly outside, Yoko had an idea. If a video camera pointed at the sky could be hooked up to a television set, the sky, not programs, could be on TV. With *Sky TV*, Yoko created one of the earliest examples of video art. She had already created numerous performance pieces and objects and seemingly countless instructions. She figured that if she was going to explore all different kinds of media, why not give filmmaking a go?

Yoko thought up *Sky TV* (1966)—a television set that broadcasts only sky—when she was having a hard time seeing through her apartment's smoked-glass windows. With *Sky TV*, she was encouraging viewers to consider an infinite world—something bigger than themselves.

Encouraged by George Maciunas, Yoko made two five-minute slow-motion black-and-white films in early 1966. One was of her eye closing and opening. The other was of a match being struck and burning down—essentially *Lighting Piece* caught on film. As with her object *Eternal Time*, she was using these films to ask viewers to reconsider what they thought was true about the passage of time. A few months later, Maciunas offered Yoko a great opportunity: "He just called me one day and said, 'I've got this machine that's extremely interesting. It's a high-speed camera and I can only use it for today and tomorrow. Just think of an idea and we'll quickly do it.' So I thought of this incredible idea of the bottoms."

Yoko was interested in breaking down taboos around the body—she had shown that with *Cut Piece*. Now she was fascinated by the idea of filming and then stringing together images of people's naked bottoms. She invited many of her Fluxus friends, including the multimedia artist Jeff Perkins, to her apartment on West One Hundredth Street to participate. Perkins remembered the atmosphere as being one of pure adventure: "Some of the [participants] knew Yoko and were admirers, or at least co-conspirators. A few of my friends who did it were not artists and really had no idea what was going on, but simply did it because they thought it was funny."

Under Yoko's direction, Perkins filmed the volunteers' rear ends as, one by one, they walked the fifteen steps or so from the living room to Yoko and Tony's bedroom. (Yoko and Tony also lent their bottoms to the cause.) To keep the bottoms in close-up, Perkins squatted on a hand truck—a two-wheeled device with handles that's often used in warehouses to move boxes—and then Tony would push him across the floor.

After Yoko spliced together the images of the different rear ends, each of which got between ten and fifteen seconds of screen time, she had more than five minutes of black-and-white film of bottoms in motion. Throughout the film, the screen is basically divided into four moving, even rippling, sections: two buttocks and two thighs. Yoko noticed something interesting: At such close range and seen from behind, the male and female bodies are almost indistinguishable.

The film, which Yoko arbitrarily titled *No. 4*, became an underground hit in New York and came to be known by its unofficial name: *Bottoms*. Some viewers thought it was enthrallingly bizarre. Others found the steady projection of undulating rear ends mesmerizing. Still others didn't know what to make of it but were glad to have seen the film that everyone was talking about.

Yoko had been hoping to try out her ideas in Europe eventually, and it was in large part because of *Bottoms'* success that she was invited to London in September 1966 to participate in a gathering of international artists at the Destruction in Art Symposium. In London, Yoko made an eighty-minute version of *Bottoms* starring literally hundreds of rear ends.

To an extent, she was making the *Bottoms* films to force viewers to face their anxiety about nudity, and maybe she would even coax a chuckle out of them in the process. But there was more to it. Whatever our gender, age, skin color, nationality, or social class, she felt, we all share at least one common (if rarely seen) trait, and our anatomy and vulnerability link us together. Given this, shouldn't we all treat one another as equals? If we did, wouldn't that be the end of war? As the film critic J. Hoberman put it, the second *Bottoms* film was "publicized as a peace petition that 365 people had 'signed' with their bare rumps."

Evening News

Carmelite House, Carmelite Street, E.C.4.

10 MAR 1967

WHAT'S WRONG WITH THIS ← PICTURE

Twenty - five - year - old Japanese actress Yoko Ono led a protest today against the banning of her film about the human posterior.

With several of the film's cast (unpaid) she picketed the censor's office in Soho Square and laid flowers on the door-step.

Her husband, 30-year-old director Anthony Cox, was there, too — armed with a 3ft blown-up segment of the film showing the nether portions of some anonymous anatomy.

The marchers, all eight of them, paraded defiantly along the pavement, watched with tolerant amusement by a handful of police.

Said Miss Ono: "This is not a great leg pull on my part. It was a serious film, and I hope the censor will change his mind and allow us to show it publicly. I have challenged him to appear on TV and discuss it."

The film is called "Number Four" and is a 90-minute study of naked bottoms.

Censor Mr. John Trevelyan refused to issue a certificate and asked her to remove it "as soon as possible from the premises."

To Yoko's befuddlement, her newer *Bottoms* film was banned by the British Board of Film Censors because it was considered obscene and "not suitable for public exhibition," which of course only made people want to see it more. A scheduled screening at London's Royal Albert Hall, which "accommodates six thousand bottoms," as one newspaper wryly put it, was canceled.

Yoko, Tony, and some friends and film participants staged a peaceful demonstration, handing out flowers to passersby. The normally humorless film board was charmed. After its secretary met with Yoko and Tony, the board gave in, granting the film a "mature" rating certificate. When *Bottoms* was finally screened at London's Jacey Tatler Cinema, it registered the theater's third-highest box-office sales to date.

But all this publicity put Yoko in another troubling situation: Her newly acquired fame was creating a painful distance between herself and the people around her. The more well-known she became, the more she felt shunned by those she had considered her friends. "It was coming to a point where even the generous avant-garde artists of London started saying, 'We can't invite her to dinner because she's getting too famous,'" Yoko said. "They thought I was selling out."

Not only did Yoko feel cast aside by people she thought she could count on, but she and Tony, even while living under the same roof and working and raising a child together, were drifting apart. She regarded this period as "the loneliest time in my life."

Her loneliness was about to end. ▪

OPPOSITE In response to the ban on her film *Bottoms*, Yoko, puzzled by all the fuss, told a reporter, "It's quite harmless. There's no murder or violence in it. Why shouldn't it be given a certificate?"

THE AVANT-GARDIST AND THE POP STAR

GARDIST AND THE POP STAR

(1966–1968)

A dream you dream alone is only a dream.
A dream you dream together is reality.

—YOKO ONO, 1972

John Lennon was lost. His band, the Beatles, was the most popular rock group in the world, making him one of the most famous people on earth—and putting him under terrific pressure to hold on to that title by continuing to churn out hit songs and records. But disagreements among the four bandmates were calling the group's future into question. At the same time, its fans' obsessiveness—known as Beatlemania—was making it impossible for the musicians to walk down the street without attracting attention, not to mention do what they loved: perform music in public. They couldn't hear themselves play over the roar of screaming Beatlemaniacs.

Meanwhile, John, the bespectacled Beatle considered the group's "intellectual," was in the doghouse with some members of the public for being outspoken on political issues. All four band members, but especially John and Beatles guitarist George Harrison, opposed the United States' role in the Vietnam War, which had escalated throughout the 1960s. America's position was that it was dropping bombs on the Southeast Asian country to stop the spread of communism, but it was killing a lot of innocent Vietnamese in the process. Many people—John and George among them—felt that the United States had no business getting involved in Vietnam's political struggle. John wanted to give voice to his opinion, but as a Beatle, he was expected to be squeaky-clean, which meant staying politically neutral.

Everything suddenly seemed to be going badly for John. He had no idea how to fix what was wrong with his life. What's more, his marriage to Cynthia Lennon—the mother of his three-year-old son, Julian—wasn't giving him what he felt he needed.

IN 1966, SWINGING London, as it was called, was the center of a cultural revolution focused on innovations in art, music, film, photography, and fashion. The British economy had finally recovered from World War II, and the capital city was attracting counterculturally minded people from all over the world. Men's hair was getting long and shaggy. Women's clothing was getting skimpy. As far as the city's cultural icons went, the only thing that beat out the miniskirt was the Beatles.

When John wasn't in the recording studio, he had taken to going to London art galleries. He went in part out of boredom: Since the Beatles had stopped touring, he had a lot of time on his hands. Staying at home in the suburbs with Cynthia and Julian made him feel antsy, and he escaped into drugs, which were prevalent in the rock scene. But he also visited galleries out of genuine curiosity and a desire to get back in touch with his younger, happier self: He had been attending art school when the band that would become the Beatles got together.

That autumn, Yoko had been invited to put on a solo show at London's Indica Gallery. Conceptual-art shows were going on in galleries in Germany and Italy, and this was one of London's first exhibitions of the kind. Yoko's reputation for being what many considered eccentric preceded her. John recalled, "I got the word that this amazing woman was putting on a show . . . something about people in bags, in black bags, and it was going to be a bit of a happening."

On November 9, the night Yoko's exhibition was to officially open, John attended a preview of her show, which she had titled *Unfinished Paintings and Objects by Yoko Ono.* "I was . . . astounded," he said. "There was an apple [sitting on a pedestal] on sale there for two hundred quid; I thought it was

When John Lennon saw Yoko's piece *Apple* (1966) at Indica Gallery, he got the humor in the idea of holding up a piece of fruit as a valuable work of art. To be part of the joke, he took a bite out of the apple right in front of Yoko. She thought it best to stay cool, but it wasn't easy. Later she admitted, "I was very upset at the time."

fantastic—I got the humor in her work immediately. I didn't have to have much knowledge about avant-garde or underground art, but the humor got me straightaway. It was two hundred quid to watch the fresh apple decompose." To show his appreciation, John took a bite of the apple right in front of Yoko. He gave her a mischievous little grin and then replaced the apple on its stand. Yoko was aghast.

As much as John liked the apple, it was another piece that sold him on the artist. *Ceiling Painting (YES Painting)* consisted of a white ladder positioned under a white canvas fixed to the ceiling. Hanging from the ceiling was a chain, and at the end of it was a magnifying glass. "I climbed the ladder, looked through the spyglass, and in tiny little letters it said 'yes,'" John said. "So it was positive. I felt relieved. It's a great relief when you get up the ladder and you look through the spyglass and it doesn't say 'no.'" This "yes" became a good omen for their relationship and fit perfectly with Yoko's line of thinking when she created the piece: "I was an outcast in the avant-garde because the rest of the avant-garde was trying to alienate the audience . . . I was trying to communicate. I was trying to say 'love' and 'peace' and 'yes.'"

John found it refreshing that Yoko didn't seem to recognize his face. "She came up and handed me a card that said 'breathe' on it—one of her instructions." John moved very close to her so that she could hear him breathing. She was startled but tried not to show it.

Yoko and John were finally introduced by the gallery's owner, who was a friend of John's. Although John liked to think of himself as edgy, Yoko saw standing before her "a clean-cut man with his own elegance." She was about as familiar with John's work as he was with hers. "I was an underground person, and such an artistic snob," she said later. "I knew about the Beatles, of course . . . but I wasn't interested in them." Just about the only thing she could recall about them was drummer Ringo Starr's first name, because *ringo* means "apple" in Japanese.

John also liked Yoko's *Ceiling Painting (YES Painting)* (1966) when he saw it at Indica Gallery. Even though Yoko would exhibit the piece over the years, she couldn't let gallerygoers continue to physically interact with it: It wouldn't survive all the traffic up and down its ladder. But she figured people could still interact with it with their minds.

Then John caught sight of Yoko's instruction *Painting to Hammer a Nail*. It read,

> Hammer a nail into a mirror, a piece of glass, a canvas, wood or metal every morning. Also, pick up a hair that came off when you combed in the morning and tie it around the hammered nail. The painting ends when the surface is covered with nails.

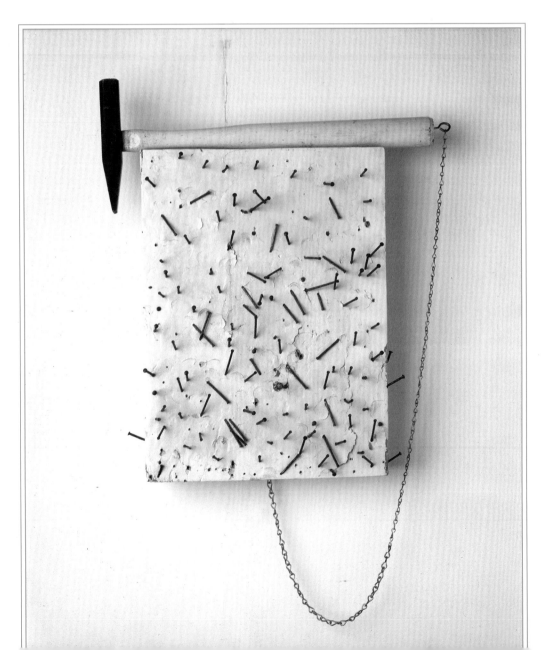

Yoko had provided a canvas-size wood panel that she had painted white. A hammer dangled by a chain attached to the panel. A jar of nails sat on a chair beneath it. Once the show officially opened, visitors would be free to hammer nails into the panel.

Painting to Hammer a Nail tantalized John. He asked Yoko if he could drive in its first nail. She told him to forget it: The show hadn't yet opened, and she wanted the piece to be untouched until then. The gallery's owner couldn't believe what he was hearing. John later said, "The owner whispered to her, 'Let him hammer a nail in. You know, he's a millionaire. He might buy it.'"

Yoko thought they were both pretty nervy. She had an idea: "I said it was all right if he pays five shillings." John had a ready answer: Instead of paying five shillings, could he just hammer an imaginary nail? Yoko later wrote, "I thought, so I met a guy who plays the same game I played." "That's when we really met," John said. "That's when we locked eyes and she got it and I got it and, as they say in all the interviews we do, the rest is history."

Not quite. Their minds may have met, but each was married, and it would be some time before they could really get to know each other.

Yoko's Indica Gallery show spoke to people besides John. One critic wrote that the exhibition might "provide an important first step towards finding our way back to the world of imagination and fantasy." Yoko was pleased by the good press, but it wasn't her only takeaway from the show. She didn't forget the man she had connected with there.

After catching his eye at another artist's opening a few weeks later, Yoko sent a copy of *Grapefruit* to John at Abbey

For her *Half-A-Wind* show at Lisson Gallery, Yoko created *Half-A-Room* (1967) in response to the feeling that "there was a half empty space in my life": She and Tony were growing apart. "Somebody said I should also put half-a-person in the show," she wrote at the time. "But we are halves already."

Road, the Beatles' recording studios. His initial reaction to it was mixed: "Sometimes I'd get very annoyed by it; it would say things like 'paint until you drop dead' or 'bleed.' Then sometimes I'd be very enlightened by it. I went through all the changes that people go through with her work—sometimes I'd have it by the bed and I'd open it and it would say something nice and it would be all right, and then it would say something heavy and I wouldn't like it." But by then it was fair to say that Yoko had made an indelible impression on him.

YOKO, WITH THE help of Tony and some local art students, got busy working on pieces that would appear in her *Half-A-Wind* show, which opened in October 1967 at Lisson Gallery. For a piece called *Half-A-Room*, she exhibited various everyday objects—a chair, a table, a bed, a rug, a teapot, a hat—that had been cut in half and painted white and then arranged in what looked like a one-room domestic setting. White was becoming an important feature of her art. She felt that viewers could freely imagine projecting their own colors onto it.

Three Spoons (1967), which Yoko also exhibited at Lisson Gallery, had a contradictory title: There are four, not three, spoons on display. As with *Half-A-Room*, Yoko was asking viewers to reconsider what they thought they knew to be true about material objects.

In addition to "bagism," as Yoko came to think of her events in bags, she had many performance pieces in which she hid or concealed something (or someone). Now, with her half objects, instead of hiding or concealing things, she was taking away parts of them. With all these pieces, she was hoping that viewers would question the value of using their senses—especially sight and touch—to navigate the world when memory or imagination can simply fill in the blanks, maybe in a more interesting way.

But the half objects weren't just a mental exercise: Yoko's personal life had inspired them. "Tony and I were not getting along anymore," she explained. "Every night Tony wasn't coming back, and one morning I woke up and there was a big space on the other side of the bed. So, I thought, 'Half-a-bed, that's interesting.' And then I started thinking about half-an-object … I realized that there was a half empty space in my life." It was not yet clear that John was meant to fill the other half.

When the *Half-A-Wind* show was still in its planning stage, Yoko decided to phone John at Abbey Road to tell him that John Cage was in London. Cage, she said, was compiling a book of twentieth-century music scores and hoped that the Beatles would contribute to it. John, keen to hear more, invited Yoko to the studio that night to talk.

She was happy to have the opportunity to get to know him better. By now she had read and admired John's two published books of poetic nonsense verse and prose, which he had illustrated with playful line drawings. The books showed off his absurd sense of humor, which also came out in Beatles songs with odd and funny titles like "I Am the Walrus" and "Mean Mr. Mustard" and "Help!" And John's writing, full of whimsical statements ("It was little Bobby's birthmark today"), reminded Yoko of her own.

Yoko came to the studio, and during the band's break, John told her that he liked *Grapefruit* and asked when he could see more of her work. Yoko told him about her half objects. The concept floored him. On the spot, he offered to sponsor her show, which needed financing. She was elated, of course, but felt that "there was something sad about making John Lennon be an art patron, when he was such a brilliant artist himself." After she suggested that he contribute something to the show, "John looked up at the ceiling and immediately said, 'How about putting the other halves in bottles?' Just like that. It was beautiful. So his bottles with labels like 'the other half of a chair,' et cetera, were exhibited on a shelf in the gallery where I had my half objects." John's bottles were empty, but viewers could imagine them filled with the halves missing from Yoko's incomplete objects.

Yoko subtitled her *Half-A-Wind* show *Yoko Plus Me*. The

OPPOSITE Yoko's *A Box of Smile* (1967) is a small, square hinged box that fits in the hand. Lifting the lid reveals a mirror at the bottom of the box. Yoko wanted the piece to both inspire a smile and reassure the person holding it that happiness is within reach. Yoko had a smile box made as a gift for John in 1968.

"Me" was a cagey reference to John, whose role was down-played—the shelf exhibiting his bottles was simply labeled "J. L."—because Yoko thought that people might assume she was using him for his attention-grabbing name. She also didn't want people to zero in on his work and miss hers. As it turned out, John didn't even attend the well-reviewed show. "I was too uptight," he admitted later.

For a time Yoko kept in touch with John by mailing him daily instructions—she called this *Dance Event*—that said things like "Dance" and "Watch all the lights until dawn" and "I'm a cloud. Watch for me in the sky." John found the instructions as perplexing as he found them intriguing.

Yoko and John began to hang out, and their feelings for each other grew. One night in May 1968, when Cynthia was vacationing in Greece and Julian was staying with the Lennons' housekeeper, John sensed that if he and Yoko were meant to be together, this was his chance to find out. With some trepidation, he telephoned her at her London apartment and invited her to his house outside the city. She was flattered by the gesture, thinking it was an invitation to a party, and agreed to come. John sent his chauffeur-driven Rolls-Royce to fetch her. It was a luxury of a kind that Yoko hadn't known since her childhood.

But there wasn't a party, she realized: It was just the two of them. At first they both felt shy. To break the tension, John resorted to what he knew best. "I played her all the tapes that I'd made," he said later, "all this far-out stuff, some comedy stuff, and some electronic music. There were very few people I could play those tapes to." Yoko knew exactly what John was going through. "He was . . . feeling like a lonely artist because he was being told by people around him, 'That is not good; it's a bit too crazy.' . . . He asked [me], 'Is this all right?' [after]

he brought out these cassettes. I'd say, 'Are you kidding? This is beautiful.'" Finally she said to John, "Well, let's make one ourselves."

They stayed up all night in John's home studio, talking and working on an experimental musical collaboration. By then Yoko knew that she was in love with him and that he felt the same. When they were done making music, they made love. For both, it felt as though a window that had been sealed shut for years had been yanked wide open. John remembered, "I had no doubt I'd met The One."

In June, John moved out of his big house and into a one-bedroom apartment in London's Montagu Square. Although it pained her to be away from Kyoko, Yoko moved in with him. Julian stayed at the house with Cynthia, and Kyoko stayed with Tony. Yoko and John both filed for divorce.

On a superficial level, Yoko and John were an unlikely couple. True, they had both grown up during the bombings of World War II, and they were both artists, but her background was avant-garde, and his was rock and roll. They were born and raised half a world away from each other, she in the East by an upper-class family, he in the West by his no-nonsense upper-working-class aunt, Mimi. (John's mother, who died when he was seventeen, hadn't wanted to raise her son, and he had barely known his father.) Yoko, thirty-five when she moved in with John, was more than seven years older than the Beatle—an age gap noteworthy to people uncomfortable with the idea of a woman being significantly older than her partner.

But a shared sensibility can eclipse surface differences. When Yoko met John, she, too, was floundering, finding her level of fame (although on a smaller scale than his) disconcerting. John's sense of being an outsider, like Yoko's, traced back

OPPOSITE In 1968, Yoko and John participated in a group sculpture show at Coventry Cathedral in England. Their "sculpture" was two acorns, which they planted in the cathedral's garden; they called this *Acorn Event*. John told the press, "One [acorn] faced east and the other faced west, to symbolize that East and West have met through Yoko and me."

to his childhood, and both had been rebellious and branded this way early in their lives and careers. Neither Yoko nor John stuck with one form of artistic expression. Both were having trouble finding a balance between giving their art and their children—born four months apart—adequate attention. And both felt constantly misunderstood by others.

It was uncanny, really, how alike they were. Yoko had studied music but wound up being an artist; John had studied art but wound up being a musician. "Sometimes, I think that some of the things I've done could have been done by John, and vice versa," she said. As their first public act of art making as a couple, Yoko and John participated in a group sculpture show by planting two acorns in the ground, one representing each artist.

PART OF YOKO and John's mutual fascination had to do with their hunger to learn from each other. John took the task of introducing Yoko to rock and roll very seriously, and she took pride in introducing him to classical music and the world of filmmaking. One of their film collaborations was *Two Virgins*, in which for nineteen minutes the artists' faces are superimposed, shifting out of alignment, and finally merged—a comment on their perception of themselves as unified in every way.

John—spurred on by Yoko, who loved his ideas—put on his first solo art exhibition, *You Are Here*, at London's Robert Fraser Gallery in July. The conceptual show was named for the phrase printed on London subway maps to help riders get their bearings, although John had a deeper meaning in mind. The show's opening, to which Yoko and John wore their now customary white, began when they released 365 white

helium-filled balloons. John dedicated the show "To Yoko from John, with Love." He credited her with giving him the confidence to step out of his "Beatle John" straitjacket and realize his dream of exhibiting his work. "Yoko really woke me up to myself," he explained. "She didn't fall in love with the Beatles, she didn't fall in love with my fame, she fell in love with *me*, for myself. And through that she brought out the best in me—by encouraging me in my artwork, my films, and my writing, which are all things I did almost like a hobby."

Yoko was equally clear about her feelings for John. "I was just about at the vanishing point," she said. "But John came in and said, 'All right, I understand you.'" This feeling of being bonded to another person was entirely new to her. "To me John was a mountain, and I was the wind—I was just blowing around, going from one country to another without a root. By connecting with him, I became anchored."

The British press reported—often in a sneering tone—on Yoko and John's small-scale avant-garde events and films. But on November 11, 1968, *Unfinished Music No. 1: Two Virgins*, the experimental album they had made at John's house the night they became lovers, first introduced the world to what the two were capable of creating together. The public didn't like what it heard—or saw, for that matter.

Critics and fans alike were stunned. The improvised record contains nothing that can be described as songs, at least in the traditional sense. John plays guitar or piano while Yoko vocalizes abstractly, or listeners hear fragments of their conversation. John can be heard whistling; Yoko can be heard pretending to cry like a baby. The album's music was "unfinished," Yoko said—a word she had used to title her Indica Gallery show—because "if you listen to it, maybe you can add to it or change it or edit or add something in your mind. The unfinished part that's not in the record—what's in you, not what's in the record—is what's important."

But the record didn't become notorious for just what was found in its grooves. On its front cover is a black-and-white photo of the artists facing the camera, completely naked; on its back cover is a photo of them snapped from behind a few minutes later, holding hands and looking over their inside shoulders. The public was (and probably remains) under the impression that John's mysterious artist girlfriend had put him up to the stunt, but in fact the nude album cover was his idea. It caused a sensation. The record had to be distributed in a brown-paper wrapper in order to be sold in stores.

As the music critic John Rockwell interpreted the album cover, "For John and Yoko, nudity was a challenge to a stuffy and overserious society, a statement about innocence and openness, and a talisman of trust between them." John's explanation was simpler: "People have got to become aware . . . that being nude is not obscene. Being ourselves is what's important. If everyone practiced being themselves instead of pretending to be what they aren't, there would be peace."

The public had disapproved of their relationship to begin with. Yoko was denounced as a home wrecker—the same could have been said about John, although it wasn't—and viewed with extra distaste because she was a "foreigner." Now the world was convinced that it had proof of her corrupting influence on the Beatle who until then had been reliably entertaining (and reliably dressed). People were hostile in a way that the artists, who meant well, hadn't anticipated. But as Yoko and John consoled each other, their bond grew stronger. It had to, considering they'd only just begun to raise eyebrows. ▪

5

PEACE, LOVE, AND ART

(1968–1970)

"We're going to stage many happenings…
and this marriage was one of them."

—YOKO ONO, 1969

PAGE 88 Some were surprised when Yoko and John, who seemed so unconventional, did what "regular" people do and got married. "We believe in lots of rituals, and this contemporary society doesn't have very many rituals that we believe in," Yoko explained. Added John: "We believe that rituals . . . slow down the world. We think it's too fast."

The world was a far from peaceful place in 1968. The civil rights activist Martin Luther King Jr. was assassinated. So was the Democratic presidential candidate Bobby Kennedy, brother of the late U.S. president John F. Kennedy. As the Vietnam War raged, the antiwar and civil rights movements were at the height of their powers, and the women's movement was gathering steam. There were riots in Chicago at the Democratic National Convention, and college students rallied for peace on their campuses. Yoko and John were part of the youth-fueled protest against violence, oppression, and negativism, but their methods were different from most people's. Their chief weapons? Love and art.

The artists were inseparable. Soon after Yoko and John went public with their romance, the media dubbed her the "fifth Beatle"—a snide reference to John's insistence that she be present whenever the Beatles were working. Yoko gladly accompanied him to Abbey Road, where traditionally wives and girlfriends—if they showed up at all—sat on the sidelines and kept mum. Not Yoko: She was usually within whispering range of John.

Often Yoko just sat quietly, observing: The world of rock was new to her, and there was a lot to take in. Or she might knit or hang paper on the wall and paint to help pass the hours. (Recording sessions could be long and tedious.) But at other times she volunteered her opinions, which some felt she was unqualified to offer. For her, making art was about collaboration, and she didn't understand why her fellow artists might not value her input. Since Yoko didn't follow popular culture, she didn't know that the Beatles had a time-tested, near-decade-old music-making formula that their fans felt was not to be tampered with. "Yoko was naive," John admitted. "She came in and would expect to perform with [the other Beatles], like you would with any group . . . But they'd [have] a sort of coldness about it."

Yoko lent her voice to the band's 1968 album *The Beatles*. She can be heard speaking on "Revolution 9," an eight-minute sound collage made up of about thirty tape loops that John had fed—some backward—into one basic track. Yoko and John thought that "Revolution 9" was as revolutionary as its title indicated. But John's bandmates weren't surprised when listeners met the song with fairly unanimous bafflement. Who was blamed for the experiment? Not the song's composer. As with the *Two Virgins* album cover, Yoko took the heat for what was presumed to be her warping influence.

THE WORLD WAS getting used to Yoko's and John's little surprises. But what they did on March 20, 1969, was unexpected not because it was considered bizarre but because it was so conventional: They got married. As for the wedding, which took place in Gibraltar, the tiny British colony on the southern coast of Spain, it was no by-the-book affair. The bride and groom *both* dressed in white—or almost: John couldn't find a white suit, so he settled for a white jacket and tan pants. Even their footwear—white tennis shoes—matched. Their attire didn't just reflect Yoko's penchant for using white in her artwork. It also symbolized, like the other coordinated outfits the artists sometimes wore, their commitment to equality. The idea that they were equals in every way was a cornerstone of their marriage.

If the artists' marriage was a "happening," as Yoko told reporters, then their honeymoon was a circus. On March 25 the newlyweds took up residence for a week in a bed in the Amsterdam Hilton's presidential suite so that they could

To promote peace, the newlyweds conducted the weeklong *Bed-In for Peace* at the Amsterdam Hilton in 1969. The press was used to getting superficial fifteen-minute interviews with sought-after public figures like Yoko and John; this was something else entirely.

conduct *Bed-In for Peace*. (The name was a play on *be-ins*, the popular countercultural gatherings of the day.) If Yoko and John's goal was to draw the most attention possible to their cause, a Bed In was "the only way," she said. "We can't go out in [London's] Trafalgar Square because it would create a riot. We can't lead a parade or a march because of all the autograph hunters. We had to find our own way of doing it."

The couple conceived the event as "a commercial for peace," as John put it, "as opposed to a commercial for war, which was on the news every day . . . and in the newspapers . . . We thought, 'Well, why don't they have something *nice* in the newspapers?'" John had spent his life as a Beatle fighting for his privacy, but now he and Yoko were actually inviting reporters and photographers to their bedside. "Just suppose we had wanted to go to Capri for a secret honeymoon," John told a mystified public. "The press would have been bound to find out. So we thought we might as well do something constructive with the publicity."

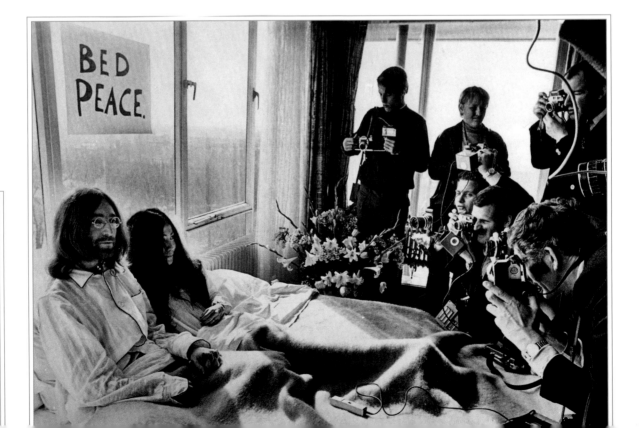

By "constructive" he meant on behalf of stopping the Vietnam War. Yoko and John were both against war on principle, but Yoko knew the horrors of war from firsthand experience. She had witnessed it, fled from it, lived through it somehow, and seen what it did to people and communities. There was no escaping the fact that being with John meant living under a spotlight. Why not make use of that spotlight by shining it on their antiwar message?

Before the Bed In started, the newlyweds told reporters, who had come to Amsterdam from all over the world, that they could ask any questions they wanted to. When the Bed In began, the hundred-odd journalists and disc jockeys and dozens of photographers may have been surprised and even disappointed by what they saw in the honeymoon bed: Yoko in a modest nightgown and John in pajamas. What's more, the couple was intent on talking about nothing juicier than the Vietnam War and peace—how to achieve it, why nonviolence was the only way to go.

Flower bouquets festooned the room, and around Yoko and John's king-size bed were their offhand drawings and hand-made signs reading BED PEACE and HAIR PEACE—a pun on what men wear on their heads to conceal their baldness. There were also quickly dashed-off signs reading I LOVE YOKO and I LOVE JOHN. "The message of peace was the strongest idea," Yoko said later, "but there was also the message of love—men and women being able to make a statement together."

Around the globe the Bed In was front-page news and a top television news story. The chatty John may have been, more often than not, the couple's mouthpiece, but he freely admitted that his soft-spoken wife was the brains behind this particular operation. "The actual peace event we staged came directly from Yoko," he said. "She had decided that whatever action she took, she took for a specific reason. Her reason was peace. I'd been singing about love, which I guess was another word for peace."

Despite their sacrifice for the common good—after all, who would want to spend their honeymoon with a parade of photographers detonating flashbulbs in their faces?—Yoko and John were treated with hostility by many reporters. The press, which Yoko felt seemed to be looking for every possible reason not to like her, made much of the fact that she so often looked serious, which some people took to mean that she was cold and invulnerable. They didn't understand that her reason for not smiling in photographs was a holdover from her childhood. As the American rock photographer Bob Gruen explained, "The American custom of saying 'cheese!' and sporting a smile is seen as very strange in Japan, where they feel life is serious, and don't want to be captured on film laughing or looking silly." And Yoko's mother had always told her that too much smiling would be taken as a sign of subservience. Yoko had long stopped believing this to be true, but she hadn't managed to completely break the habit of holding back the urge to show her feelings.

It wasn't just the press that was hostile to Yoko. One day, some of the young women who hung around outside Abbey Road in hopes of spying the Fab Four handed her a bouquet of yellow roses—thorns first. Initially, she didn't realize that this was meant to be an insult and that the color yellow was a reference to her skin color. It seemed to Yoko and John that all the press and public could focus on was her skin; her long, thick, black hair; and the shape of her eyes. Anti-Japanese sentiment left over from the war steered some people's prejudice, but this wasn't all that was going on. A particularly hateful stereotype is often used against Asian women: the "dragon lady." The dragon lady supposedly employs manipulative tricks to get what she wants—including the wealth of unsuspecting male victims.

It was odd, Yoko thought: The possibility that she could actually love John didn't seem to cross many people's minds. Her motivation for being with him was written off as a hunger for money and fame on a level that she could never reach through her fringy art. No one seemed to consider that she had something to lose—besides her privacy—in exchange for marrying one of the most famous men in the world. "Before meeting John, I was doing two concerts and lectures a month," she said. "I was in demand. I was able to express myself all the time. Suddenly, by becoming the wife of a Beatle, what was required of me was to shut up . . . I took it as a challenge, like how can I create new works in jail? It was like a prison. A strange, rare, invisible prison."

Yoko knew that there was something ironic about linking up with a man with a widely recognized name. Hadn't she spent much of her youth trying to stake out an identity beyond Ono daughter and Yasuda granddaughter?

FOR YOKO AND John, using their celebrity to publicize peace wasn't more important than making art: It *was* making art. *Bed-In for Peace* had received so much attention that in late May the couple flew to Canada for an eight-day Bed In at Montreal's Queen Elizabeth Hotel. There was all the hoped-for hoopla. The event, which Yoko and John called simply *Bed In*, was broadcast live over Canadian and U.S. radio stations. This time five-and-a-half-year-old Kyoko was on the scene. She bounced on the bed or cuddled with Yoko and John. "Bed Ins

are something that everybody can do and they're so simple," John told the rock-music magazine *Rolling Stone*. The artists would take time out to meditate or pray for peace when they weren't answering questions. Yoko wasn't religious in the traditional sense, but she did believe in using the mind to try to create change, which for her wasn't much different from praying.

On the last night of the Bed In, John picked up his acoustic guitar, which he had decorated with cartoony drawings of his and Yoko's faces. Using a far from studio-grade tape recorder, they recorded "Give Peace a Chance," which John had been inspired to write by the week's goings-on. The backing band was a diverse crew of kindred spirits, from the New York beat poet Allen Ginsberg to members of the Canadian chapter of the religious group Hare Krishna, who created a rhythm track with drums and finger cymbals. Also participating were journalists, filmmakers, photographers, friends, fans, and anyone with a guitar, including Kyoko. The song's lyrics were taped to a wall, and everyone was expected to sing the chorus: "All we are saying / is give peace a chance."

"Give Peace a Chance" would become, like John's Beatles song "All You Need Is Love," one of the peace movement's unofficial anthems. Yoko's "Remember Love" was the single's B side. The song, which she sings sweetly while John picks an acoustic guitar, begins, "Remember love / Remember love / Love is what it takes to sing." This was hardly the confrontational work that people were coming to expect from Yoko Ono. She thought that anyone who heard "Remember Love" would like it and be reminded that love was key to freedom. But to her chagrin, many didn't bother to turn over "Give Peace a Chance" and listen.

OPPOSITE The Amsterdam Bed In earned so much attention that two months later Yoko and John conducted another one, in Montreal. It was hard to measure what they were accomplishing: "With the Beatles, you put out a record and either it's a hit or it's a miss," John pointed out. But the artists believed that even if a Bed In couldn't stop the Vietnam War, their time was well spent because their message of peace was getting heard.

When journalists and photographers arrived at the press party for the Plastic Ono Band's "Give Peace a Chance" / "Remember Love" single, they expected to see a band. As John put it, "The band was onstage. It was just a machine with a camera pointed at them, showing *them* on the stage themselves . . . [As] the advert said, 'You are the Plastic Ono Band.'"

Yoko and John credited the single to the Plastic Ono Band—the name that the artists had decided on for their conceptual rock group. They plugged the record with the slogan "You are the Plastic Ono Band." The flesh-and-blood Plastic Ono Band, which, in keeping with the idea behind it, would have a fluid membership, first performed on September 13, 1969, at a rock-and-roll revival concert at the University of Toronto's Varsity Stadium. This was Yoko's introduction to rock concerts, and she was caught off guard by the grunginess of the backstage area, not to mention the size of the audience she would be playing to.

Audience members were caught off guard as well—by Yoko. She didn't seem to be making words—in Japanese *or* in English. Sometimes she seemed to make a long *eek* sound, as if imitating someone in a cartoon who has seen a mouse. At other times she sang a long *ow*, breaking up the sound so that her voice was the aural equivalent of a strobe light. Sometimes she served up alternating vowel sounds—*Ahh-ooh-ahh-ooh*—at lightning-speed high pitch. (It's harder than it sounds. Try repeating "A-E-I-O-U" as fast as you can in a high voice, and you'll get the general idea.) Her approach to rock music was different from most people's: "I would hear [John's] guitar and think, 'Wow, I can answer that.'" There was also the matter of singing loudly enough to be heard over it. By turning her voice into a musical instrument, she could hold her own.

Yoko's voice would sound by turns imploring, angry, vulnerable, heartbroken, enraptured—all this she could convey without words. Her point was that when emotion is distilled, words become unnecessary. "If you were drowning you wouldn't say: 'I'd like to be helped because I have just a moment to live,'" Yoko told *Rolling Stone*. "You'd say, 'Help!' but if you were more desperate you'd say, '*Eioughhhh.*'"

Many people had negative reactions to Yoko's vocal style, and most music critics reduced it to "screeching" or "screaming" and left it at that. They didn't *have* to enjoy it, of course. But critics who put down their pens and opened their ears discovered that her singing style contained traces of opera and German lieder—music that she had been exposed to in her youth—along with other kinds of music from around the world. Yoko wasn't happy about the meanness driving the relentless criticism she received for her vocal style, but she thought she understood it: "It's easier for people to listen to mechanical sounds than to listen to a woman cry out."

The male-dominated world of rock and roll was not ready for Yoko's improvisations. But all the bad press was shrugged off by John, her biggest fan: "She makes music like you've

The press met the WAR IS OVER! / IF YOU WANT IT billboard campaign with the usual skepticism, but Yoko and John did receive positive feedback and even thank-you notes from young people around the world—and not just fans—for their uplifting message. This encouragement helped the artists keep going.

never heard on earth . . . It's as important as anything [the Beatles] ever did." Although most would agree with the first statement, many weren't at all sure about the second.

Unlike most people—famous or otherwise—Yoko and John weren't interested in taking a break during the holidays. The Vietnam War wasn't stopping to celebrate Christmas in 1969, and they didn't want their peace crusade to lose momentum. In December they launched a campaign featuring the slogan "War Is Over! / If You Want It." Yoko saw it as an instruction, in a way, hinging as it did on her belief that people can bring about change with their minds.

Beginning on December 15, the couple arranged for the slogan, followed by the words "Happy Christmas from John & Yoko," to appear on thousands of posters around the world, many put up by volunteers who backed their cause. WAR IS OVER! / IF YOU WANT IT blared from billboards in twelve cities worldwide, including New York, Tokyo, London, Paris, and Montreal, in each location's primary language. (*E FINITA LA GUERRA! / SE VOI LO VOLETE*, Rome's billboard lyrically proclaimed.)

The artists saw to it that the slogan also appeared in hundreds of newspapers around the world and at a skywriting event in Toronto. The campaign's expense was significant, and John joked that he planned to send the bill to U.S. president Richard Nixon, whom many held accountable for miring the United States in a purposeless, no-win war in Vietnam.

With his mind on the headlines, John reported for Beatle duty in the new year. He was bitterly sick of being a Beatle. Yoko's company in the studio and at business meetings was the only thing that made it bearable. But it was Beatle Paul McCartney, not John, who announced to the world in April 1970 that he was officially leaving the group. John was fuming because he had wanted to make *his* announcement first: Back in the fall, he had told his bandmates and manager at a business meeting that he had had it with being a Beatle, but he'd been persuaded to keep his decision quiet for a while lest the news jeopardize a lucrative music deal in the works. With Paul's public statement half a year later, the Beatles ended.

To compound John's frustration at being beaten to the punch, Yoko was squarely blamed for the breakup: in the papers, in Beatles fan-club newsletters, on the street. For some Beatles followers it was just too painful to passively accept the news of the breakup, no matter which Beatle had initiated it, so they looked for an easy target of blame, and they didn't have to look farther than the end of John's arm to find Yoko. John was now being quite vocal about his own long-standing dissatisfaction with being a Beatle, and for some, it was inconceivable that he could just let go of being half of Lennon-McCartney— the most famous songwriting partnership of all time. They thought Yoko had exerted some kind of mind control over him—it was the dragon-lady business all over again.

Blaming her didn't make sense. "I don't think you could have broken up four very strong people like them, even if you tried," Yoko said. "The world gives me too much power," she insisted. "Only the Beatles could break up the Beatles." But Yoko knew that she had validated a side of John that the rest of the world hadn't seen—and often didn't appreciate once it saw. Yet anyone could tell that John was happier now. When he said, "Yoko's art is waking people up to their own potentialities," he was well aware that he was one of those people.

But if Yoko was key to showing John his full potential, they both knew that she was not responsible for his disillusionment with being a Beatle, which predated their first meeting. Years after the band split up, John felt compelled to explain for the umpteenth time what had gone down: "I was starting to drift from the Beatles before Yoko. What I did . . . in my own cowardly way was *use* Yoko . . . It was like now I have the strength to leave because I know there is another side to life."

Very few people tried to see John's point of view: that he felt trapped in his Beatles box, that he didn't share his bandmates' musical visions, that he could no longer grow artistically as a Beatle. Some in the Beatles' inner circle didn't stop to consider that their hostility toward Yoko might have forced John to make a choice. John told *Rolling Stone*, "It seemed that I either had to be married to [the Beatles] or Yoko. I chose Yoko . . . And I was right."

Yoko and John felt that they had it all: love, fame, money, artistic freedom, and loads of ideas. What could possibly go wrong? ▪

6

SOME TIME IN NEW YORK CITY

(1970–1973)

" No one can take you anywhere; it is your footsteps that take you to places. "

—YOKO ONO, 1972

PAGES 104–5 In August 1972, Yoko and John performed a benefit concert at Madison Square Garden. Their commitment to helping others was becoming a distraction from the mounting problems in their personal lives.

Now that John Lennon was no longer a Beatle, everyone wanted to know: What would his music—not his and Yoko's—sound like? His first solo album, the well-received *John Lennon/Plastic Ono Band*, features songs about regret, self-doubt, and losing his parents. John even threw in a few grade-A screams that made Yoko proud.

When John released the record, at the end of 1970, Yoko released its sibling, *Yoko Ono/Plastic Ono Band*. "We're both looking at the same thing from different sides of the table," John said about the twin albums' concept. "Mine is literate, hers is revolutionary." The front covers of both albums show the couple relaxing under a giant old tree at Tittenhurst Park, their mansion in the English countryside, but on Yoko's album she reclines against John, and on his their positions are reversed. They were trying to draw attention to their totally merged lives, although some cynics thought that by putting out records with nearly identical covers, the artists were trying to trick John Lennon fans into buying Yoko's album.

Rock's customary perfectionism in the studio was, Yoko felt, a waste of time. "All of these tracks were 'improvisations'—jam sessions with no rehearsal, which was what I believed music should be at the time," she later wrote. "We did not have to correct one drumbeat, one guitar note. John and I felt that together we had created a 'New Music,' a fusion of avant-garde-jazz-rock and East and West."

"I think that in 1980 music will probably sound like this," an American disc jockey said about the album shortly after its release. Yoko and John were listening to his radio show, and they thought this could be it: People might really get Yoko's sound this time. The disc jockey predicted that "there are people who are going to love it and people who are going to hate it."

For the most part they hated it. If this was rock, people wondered, where were the verses and choruses? Where were the lyrics and melodies? By now Yoko knew to expect a certain amount of hatred from the public. But she couldn't even count on her old friends for support. Some avant-garde purists, who considered rock music beneath Yoko, intimated that her marrying John Lennon was the worst thing that could have happened to her art. Yoko disagreed. "Falling in love didn't interrupt my career as an artist—it was how society dealt with it that was disruptive," she said. "The world decided I was gonna be Mrs. Lennon and nobody wanted to hear from me as an artist anymore." How could Yoko and John win? His fans felt that she was ruining his work by making it too weird, and those who admired *her* art felt that *he* was ruining it by making it too mainstream. To Yoko and John, it sometimes seemed that only they believed in each other.

To promote their twin albums, the artists traveled to New York City in late 1970. It was their first trip there as a couple. Being in New York again was exhilarating for Yoko. She had told John all about her life there and wanted badly for the city to speak to him as it did to her. He had been there before, but in Beatle capacity, which meant being all but confined to his hotel or dressing room when he wasn't onstage.

Yoko knew that the only way to really get to know Manhattan was on foot, so she got John moving. "She knew every inch," he said. "She made me walk around the streets and parks and squares and examine every nook and cranny." The city lived up to Yoko's raves, and then some. "There's an unbelievably creative atmosphere on this little island of Manhattan," John said. "It has everything you could possibly want, night and day." Best of all, the city's scale and busyness allowed Yoko

By 1970, both Yoko and John had seen quite a number of the world's major cities, but New York was the only one that seemed capable of keeping up with their pace.

and John a degree of anonymity that they wouldn't know in a smaller and less focused city. The artists were recognized, but New Yorkers were usually too preoccupied with their own lives to stop and demand an autograph or a conversation.

Although Yoko was very happy in her marriage, she ached for what was missing in her life: her daughter. She hadn't seen Kyoko since January 1970, when the girl was living in Denmark with Tony and his new wife, Melinda. But seeing Kyoko wasn't a simple matter of hopping on a plane: Tony and Melinda had moved somewhere with the girl, and they hadn't told Yoko, who hadn't initiated a formal custody arrangement with Tony, where they'd gone or how she could get in touch with them. Tony was convinced that she and John would use their money to hire lawyers who would keep Kyoko from him. This wasn't Yoko's intent at all. "I know that Tony is very close to her, and I'm not about to try to cut that relationship off," she told the *New Yorker*. All she wanted was her fair share of time with her daughter.

She had no illusions about having been a perfect parent: "I was sort of an offbeat mother, but we had very good communication. I wasn't particularly taking care of her, but she was always with me—onstage or at gallery shows . . . She was closer to my ex-husband because of that." Even so, Yoko wondered, why should that mean she didn't deserve a relationship with Kyoko at all?

In April 1971, Yoko and John, feeling helpless, hired private detectives to look all around the world for Kyoko. This was a hard decision for Yoko. She was wary of getting detectives involved: If Tony found out about them, this could escalate the tension between them. On the other hand, Yoko didn't want Kyoko to look back on her life one day and think that her mother hadn't done all she could to find her.

The detectives finally tracked down Tony, Melinda, and Kyoko in Spain, on the island of Majorca. Against her better instincts, Yoko went with her lawyer's suggestion that she and John go to Spain and physically take the child from her school—"the totally wrong thing to do, of course," Yoko said later. Understandably, Kyoko started screaming, and Yoko and John were arrested and questioned in court. There, Kyoko was given the choice of who she wanted to live with, and she chose her father. Yoko couldn't blame her.

Heartsick but resigned to giving her daughter some space after her bad judgment call, Yoko tried to resume her life with John at Tittenhurst Park. But in August, the couple moved permanently to New York. Tittenhurst was majestic but isolating, and Yoko hoped that the city would give the artists an outlet for their distress. John liked the easy access to Julian that living at Tittenhurst had given him, but he no longer had to stay in England for the good of his career.

The couple took up residence in a large suite at the St. Regis Hotel, on Manhattan's upscale Fifth Avenue. It was a far cry from Yoko's gritty downtown haunts, but she wasn't complaining: It was still New York. The antiwar movement was reaching fever pitch across the United States, and Manhattan was the nerve center of revolt. Now the artists could participate at close range. New York offered more than a chance to be at the center of the action, though. Yoko and John felt appreciated in America in a way that they didn't in Britain, with its famously scandal-mad press. Plus, in New York they didn't stand out as much as an interracial couple.

There was yet one more reason for their move to the States. Yoko had gotten word that Tony and Melinda had taken eight-year-old Kyoko to live in Melinda's hometown of Houston, Texas. Being based in the States would make it easier for Yoko to see her daughter—at least in theory.

Soon after their move to New York, the artists traveled to the United States Virgin Islands court where Yoko had gotten her divorce from Tony. After she told her story—and it was quite a story—she was awarded custody of Kyoko. But the following month, Tony persuaded a Houston judge that Yoko and John lived a rock-and-roll lifestyle that wasn't favorable to raising a child. Since the Virgin Islands ruling was still pending, Yoko lost custody of Kyoko. She was given visiting rights, including at Christmas. This wasn't much consolation: Christmas was months away. Yoko's sadness guided her waking hours and infiltrated her dreams.

THAT FALL, JOHN released *Imagine*, the solo album he had recorded that summer at Tittenhurst. The record's single, his idealistic "Imagine," was inspired by Yoko's use of the word in her instructions—"Imagine your head filled with pencil leads," "Imagine letting a goldfish swim across the sky," and so on. Yoko couldn't help feeling hurt that John hadn't acknowledged her contribution anywhere on his album. How could he be miffed that the world wasn't giving her credit for being an important artist if he wasn't either? Later John, feeling contrite, said, "Actually that should be credited as a Lennon-Ono song because a lot of it—the lyric and the concept—came from Yoko. But those days I was a bit more selfish, a bit more macho, and I sort of omitted to mention her contribution. But it was right out of *Grapefruit*, her book."

Yoko had also been busy recording music at Tittenhurst, and once again, she released a solo album in tandem with John's. *FLY*—the name of her 1964 performance piece and her 1970 film about female objectification, in which a camera tracks a fly as it grazes on the body of a nude woman—was now the name of a double record. This time around she had created some straight-ahead pop and rock songs. She modeled "Midsummer New York" on the 1950s rock classic "Heartbreak

In *FLY*, Yoko's twenty-five-minute 1970 film, a camera tracks a fly as it grazes on the body of a nude woman lying completely still. Yoko was highlighting the way that the female body is so often objectified, and she hoped that her film would encourage women not to lie back and take it anymore.

Hotel," which had been popularized by John's boyhood idol, Elvis Presley. Yoko's joke was that Presley's satiny, affected vocal style couldn't be more different from her unbridled, spontaneous approach to singing. But there was no danger of people concluding that by paying tribute to Elvis, Yoko was going mainstream. She put plenty of curiosities on the record, including "Toilet Piece/Unknown"—thirty seconds of toilet flushing.

Although some of FLY's songs had real commercial potential, Yoko's record company, presuming a lack of interest from music buyers, did little to promote it. One of FLY's songs, Yoko's autobiographical ballad "Mrs. Lennon," was about exactly this phenomenon: No matter what she called herself or created, the public still defined her first and foremost as an ex-Beatle's wife, and it didn't think it needed to know any more about her. As John put it, she was the world's most famous unknown artist: "Everybody knows her name, but nobody knows what she does."

But there was one world in which Yoko was better known for her work than for her mate. Somehow during all the excitement and tumult of moving to New York and fighting for her right to see Kyoko, she found time and energy to put together a retrospective of her artwork. Fortunately, she had created a lot of art. It would take over three floors and even the bathrooms of the venue that had invited her: the Everson Museum of Art, in Syracuse, New York.

Yoko wanted the show to open on October 9, 1971—John's thirty-first birthday. The retrospective—something of a rarity for a woman in the United States at this time—would be her gift to him. Remembering how thrilled John had been to have his own solo exhibition in London a few years earlier, Yoko named him "guest artist" on her show's press release. She titled her retrospective *This Is Not Here*—her coy answer to *You Are Here*, the name of John's solo show.

More than five thousand people came out in the rain on opening day, some dying to see Yoko's work but a predictable faction, aware that John would be present, primarily there to stargaze. During one of the press conferences before the show's opening, Yoko had said that she hoped to receive some "really serious criticism." She was referring to the fact that since she began her romance with a Beatle, she had received a lot more feedback on her looks and personality than on her work. To her immense gratification, the show was written up in major national art magazines and praised for its versatility and originality.

Water Event was part of *This Is Not Here*, Yoko's 1971 retrospective at the Everson Museum of Art. She sent out invitations requesting that people contribute something—anything—to do with water. Yoko's idea was to draw attention to what all human beings have in common—after all, everyone's body is about two-thirds water.

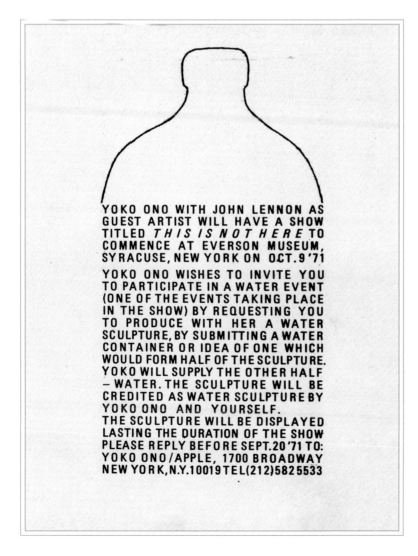

YOKO ONO WITH JOHN LENNON AS GUEST ARTIST WILL HAVE A SHOW TITLED *THIS IS NOT HERE* TO COMMENCE AT EVERSON MUSEUM, SYRACUSE, NEW YORK ON OCT. 9 '71

YOKO ONO WISHES TO INVITE YOU TO PARTICIPATE IN A WATER EVENT (ONE OF THE EVENTS TAKING PLACE IN THE SHOW) BY REQUESTING YOU TO PRODUCE WITH HER A WATER SCULPTURE, BY SUBMITTING A WATER CONTAINER OR IDEA OF ONE WHICH WOULD FORM HALF OF THE SCULPTURE. YOKO WILL SUPPLY THE OTHER HALF — WATER. THE SCULPTURE WILL BE CREDITED AS WATER SCULPTURE BY YOKO ONO AND YOURSELF. THE SCULPTURE WILL BE DISPLAYED LASTING THE DURATION OF THE SHOW PLEASE REPLY BEFORE SEPT. 20 '71 TO: YOKO ONO / APPLE, 1700 BROADWAY NEW YORK, N.Y. 10019 TEL (212) 582 5533

Despite the accolades, Yoko decided to slide art making onto the back burner after the show opened. She was so committed to her marriage of equals that she thought it best to put music making and political activism—both of which accommodated collaboration better—front and center.

While living in midtown at the St. Regis Hotel, Yoko and John decided that they needed some space to call their own. Now the face of bohemia in downtown's Greenwich Village was not just beatniks but also hippies: young people who tended to wear their hair long, listen to rock music, use drugs recreationally, and speak out against the war. The artists found a two-room apartment in the Village, at 105 Bank Street, that became a bustling center of activism. Among their many well-known neighbors was folk icon Bob Dylan, and among their many visitors—some lucky enough to enjoy one of Yoko's home-cooked macrobiotic meals—were Allen Ginsberg, the poet who had been at the Montreal Bed In, and Bobby Seale, the chairman of the black activist group the Black Panther Party.

Given all this activity, the idea of Yoko and John just blending in with the neighborhood seemed pretty laughable. But for the most part their neighbors let them be. The artists sure didn't dress like flamboyant rock stars: They favored jeans with a turtleneck (for Yoko) or a T-shirt (for John). On weekends they sent home their hired help and split dish duty and any other unavoidable housework. They bought bicycles and rode them around Greenwich Village, went to the movies in the wee hours of the night, did their own shopping, and walked to the newsstand to pick up the Sunday paper. "People don't grab us when we walk in the Village," Yoko said. "They sort of smile from a distance, which is nice."

OPPOSITE For *Add Color Painting*, Yoko supplied canvases or wall-mounted boards and brushes and colorful paints with which viewers could leave their mark. "All people are artists," she insisted. "It's just that some people think they are not because they have been told by society they are not."

Not everyone who smiled or looked at them on the street meant well. Because of John's influence and left-leaning political affiliations, the Federal Bureau of Investigation (FBI) had opened a file on him in which agents kept track of his and Yoko's every move. Yoko and John were under surveillance.

IN DECEMBER 1971, Yoko and John set off to spend Christmas with Kyoko, in accordance with Yoko's visitation rights. They arrived on the agreed-upon date at the Houston courthouse where Tony was to bring the child. But he refused to let them see Kyoko except in his presence. There was only so much Yoko's lawyers could do: Tony and Melinda disappeared with Kyoko on Christmas Eve.

Yoko was undone. She and John launched a massive search for Kyoko. They had to stay put, though: Their fame was so great that every local paper and news broadcast would report on any visit the couple made, and this could reach Tony, who would surely flee once again with the already beleaguered child. Yoko resisted the urge to file kidnapping charges against him with the U.S. government. "Kyoko has had enough traumatic experiences without the police coming to grab her father," she explained.

Her agony over missing Kyoko and her knowledge that the girl had to be missing her mother left Yoko jittery and teary. As usual, she was grateful for the distraction of work—in this case, political activism. She and John entered 1972 more committed than ever to giving—their assets, popularity, time—to causes they believed in. They were mulling over the idea of a get-out-the-vote tour. Nixon was gearing up for his November reelection bid, and this would be the first presidential election when eighteen-year-olds, known for their enthusiasm for rock music and its creators, were allowed to vote.

Meanwhile, Nixon and his people wondered: Could the artists influence the results of a presidential election? The president and his increasingly anxious administration feared that the couple might try to disrupt the Republican National Convention, at that time slated to be held in San Diego in August. The FBI agents sharpened their pencils and continued their search for evidence that John and Yoko were a threat to the country's security.

The agents never could have guessed that keeping tabs on the couple would require daytime-TV viewing. But from February 14 through 18, 1972, there were Yoko and John, minding their manners on a bland, top-rated program, *The Mike Douglas Show*. They had been guests on highbrow late-night talk shows, but daytime television was something else. They would be reaching Middle America, especially white, middle-class, stay-at-home moms and senior citizens.

OPPOSITE Yoko and John understood the importance of relaxing, as they did at the St. Moritz Hotel in New York City in 1972. Despite the hustle and bustle of their lives, they made sure to find time for just the two of them.

6 SOME TIME IN NEW YORK CITY

OPPOSITE To promote her 1971 one-woman show—"show" in the conceptual sense—Yoko's advertisement featured a photo of the entrance to the esteemed Museum of Modern Art. Yoko can be seen walking on the sidewalk with a big white shopping bag bearing a large letter *F*; the letter is underneath the "art" in the museum's name. How could anyone say that Yoko Ono was too serious?

The Philadelphia-based *Mike Douglas Show*'s talent department had sought out the artists. They were often in the news because of their activism, events, and other public appearances, and their cohosting the show would mean a ratings bonanza, plus it might win Douglas some younger viewers. Yoko and especially TV enthusiast John had watched Douglas's show and agreed that they would feel comfortable working with the affable, disarming host. Yoko and John were told that they could choose half of the week's guests. They had a single criterion: "Everybody that we selected is participating in efforts to change the world," Yoko said. When they weren't interviewing their guests, who included musicians and activists, alongside Douglas, Yoko and John performed music backed by their band of choice, New York's Elephant's Memory. And Yoko's work—she presented some of her events—got its largest audience to date.

The week of shows with Yoko and John was among the highest rated in *The Mike Douglas Show*'s two-decade run. The experience was also a positive, if exhausting, one for the artists. When Douglas asked them on camera their immediate plans upon leaving the show, John deadpanned, "Recover."

It wouldn't be easy for them to relax. For a little while now, Yoko and John were sure that they were being watched. They often had this sensation when they left or returned to their Bank Street apartment. "I'd open the door and there'd be guys standing on the other side of the street," John said. "I'd get in the car and they'd be following me and not hiding . . . They wanted me to see I was being followed." Yoko and John also suspected that their home was bugged and that their phone lines were tapped.

The artists didn't expect the Nixon administration to be happy about their antiwar stance, but the last thing they

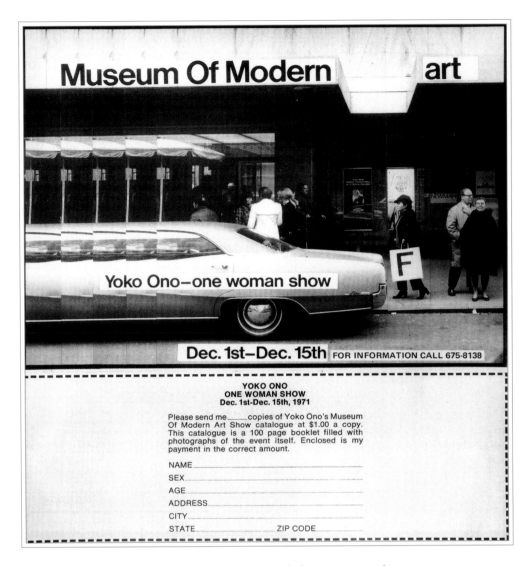

YOKO ONO
ONE WOMAN SHOW
Dec. 1st-Dec. 15th, 1971

Please send me_____copies of Yoko Ono's Museum
Of Modern Art Show catalogue at $1.00 a copy.
This catalogue is a 100 page booklet filled with
photographs of the event itself. Enclosed is my
payment in the correct amount.

NAME_____

SEX_____

AGE_____

ADDRESS_____

CITY_____

STATE_____ZIP CODE_____

wanted was to be viewed as enemies of the country they
were hell-bent on staying in. They desperately wanted an
extension on their temporary visas, which they knew were
due to expire in February 1972. If they had to leave New York
and weren't allowed back in, their ongoing search for Kyoko
would be hindered.

Anticipating trouble, Yoko and John had hired the top-
notch immigration lawyer Leon Wildes in January. It was a
smart move. A few weeks after *The Mike Douglas Show* episodes aired, the United States Immigration and Naturaliza-
tion Service (INS), nudged by the Nixon administration, sent
officers to 105 Bank Street to slide a deportation order under

the couple's door. The reason? The INS said that John had been admitted into the United States improperly, because of his 1968 bust in England for possession of marijuana. In an attempt to keep things simple, John had pleaded guilty and paid the fine. But he had always insisted that he had been framed. (Subsequent events backed him up.)

To Yoko and John, the INS's case was preposterous. There were plenty of non-Americans living freely in their midst who had the same minor drug conviction as John but weren't being threatened with deportation. Obviously, the INS was grasping at straws because the FBI hadn't come up with anything to hold against the artists: They hadn't broken any laws with their activism, hadn't incited violence or supported any violent causes—in fact, they were world-famous pacifists. The couple had complete faith that Wildes would sort out the matter, but the pressure of waiting was intense. John began smoking and drinking more. Yoko, already torn up because she couldn't find, much less see, Kyoko, found herself in a near constant state of agitation.

Leon Wildes finally managed to secure an extension on Yoko's and John's temporary visas, but the matter was far from resolved. Resigned not to be intimidated by the government's efforts to make them leave, the artists, backed by Elephant's Memory, released a Plastic Ono Band double album in June that collected their new, unabashedly political work.

Critics generally panned the album. They said that it was full of slogans, not songs. *Some Time in New York City* was "the album that ruined John's career," Yoko said later. "For John, not to be in the Top 40 was a terrible failure." She had long ago made her peace with bad press, but John still hadn't. And for once the critics couldn't blame his shortcomings on his wife.

Because of the threat of deportation, the artists felt that they had to cool it in terms of keeping company with political activists Bank Street was no longer a drop-in center for the city's antiwar contingent. So much for the national get-out-the-vote tour to defeat President Nixon. Between not knowing where Kyoko was and not knowing if they were going to get to stay in the United States, Yoko and John were stressed to the max. The couple would try to relax by watching television, but the sight of a child on the TV screen was more than Yoko could bear. John knew to quickly change the channel.

It was also discouraging that as the presidential election neared, the polls showed Nixon far ahead of his challenger, the South Dakota antiwar senator George McGovern, whom many Americans viewed as too liberal. The FBI may have undertaken a massive investigation of the artists' actions, but Yoko and John noted the cruel irony that their antiwar work didn't seem to be making a difference.

Richard Nixon was easily reelected in November 1972. It was all too much for John: the threat of deportation, the search for Kyoko, the lukewarm response to his post-Beatles career, his inability to convince the world of Nixon's wrongheadedness. John arrived drunk at an election-night party that he and Yoko attended at a Greenwich Village apartment—the left had hoped to celebrate McGovern's ouster of "Tricky Dick" Nixon—and he went into the bedroom with one of the female guests. "They started to make love, and we could all hear it," Yoko said later. "And I was just frozen, stuck there, sitting."

Out of kindness toward her, someone put on a record; everyone hoped the music would mask the unmistakable sounds of John having sex with another woman. The apartment's walls were paper-thin, so the record didn't help much. Not knowing what to do, Yoko continued to sit there, in shock. She wrote

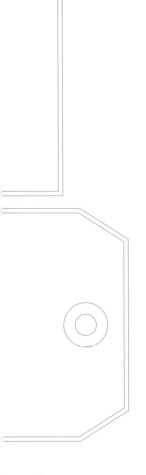

about what happened that night in the song "Death of Saman-tha." In the slow, smoky ballad, she sings several times that "something inside me / died that day."

While John continued to flounder, Yoko was starting to be recognized as a trailblazing feminist. In February she had writ-ten a widely read essay, "The Feminization of Society," for the *New York Times*. *FLY* was being heralded as a seminal femi-nist film by the day's growing number of female filmmakers.

Yoko and John decided to advertise their commitment to peace on April 1, 1973—April Fools' Day. During their press conference, the artists suddenly whipped out white handkerchiefs—the white flags of "surrender to peace," in Yoko's words—and waved them around. This was the national flag of what they called Nutopia, a conceptual country that they said they were founding.

And in 1973 she released two new and respected (at least by those who gave them a chance) women's-liberation-themed rock records.

While Yoko's creativity seemed to run on a battery that never needed recharging, John feared that his well had run dry. It made him irritable, envious, and not much fun to be around. For the first time since they fell in love, Yoko needed some space. ∎

7

REAL LIFE

(1973–1980)

It was more important to face ourselves and face that reality than to continue a life of rock 'n' roll show biz.

—JOHN LENNON, 1980

PAGES 124–25 In 1974, when Yoko and John were separated, she went to Japan to promote her solo album *Feeling the Space*; it was her first solo tour. It felt odd to be onstage without John, but for now it also felt right.

Back in June 1972, U.S. president Richard Nixon, a Republican, had OK'd a break-in at the Democratic Party's National Committee headquarters, located in the Watergate Hotel in Washington, D.C. Nixon's people planted telephone bugs and photographed documents and other privileged information. The trespassers were caught, but Nixon denied any involvement in the incident. The scandal that developed, which came to be known as Watergate, was a national embarrassment—and a national obsession.

The following May a special committee put together by the U.S. Senate began public hearings in Washington. The proceedings were televised, and in New York, Yoko and John were glued to the TV. They even traveled to D.C. to attend some of the hearings. The artists sat quietly in the balcony, hoping not to attract attention. They wanted to see the Nixon administration squirm. The administration hadn't just perpetrated a war that they—and more and more of the American people—opposed. It had caused the couple immeasurable stress during its year-plus effort to deport John. And he *still* hadn't won his case.

The artists wouldn't be together to celebrate in August 1974, when Nixon, buckling under public pressure, would resign in disgrace. In the fall of 1973, at Yoko's request, she and John separated. She hadn't forgotten his indiscretion, but that wasn't the entire reason. The truth was, John had become extremely difficult to live with. He had been dealing with his creative lull by drinking, secluding himself in the bedroom, and wallowing in self-pity. He thought his best days were behind him. Sometimes Yoko couldn't help feeling partly responsible for his gloom: Before they began collaborating, his music had gotten good reviews and sold well. She wanted him to revisit life without her and see how he liked it. They had spent literally almost every moment of the past five years together. She wanted to stop being Mrs. Lennon, if only for a little while.

At Yoko's suggestion, John moved to Los Angeles, the American rock- and movie-star capital. "It was like being sent to the desert," he said. "I had to settle things within myself." Meanwhile, Yoko stayed in New York in the couple's new home. It had to happen someday: The artists had finally outgrown their two rooms on Bank Street. In the spring of 1973, Yoko and John had moved from Greenwich Village to Manhattan's upscale but not uptight Upper West Side. They had bought an apartment on the seventh floor of the Dakota, the Gothic-style, gargoyle-studded building on the corner of West Seventy-second Street and Central Park West that had a history of celebrity tenants.

Although it would last more than a year, John liked to call his time away from Yoko his "lost weekend." The phrase reflects his drink-addled state during much of the separation, not to mention his despair.

The photogenic Dakota, into which Yoko and John moved in the spring of 1973, was featured in 1968's cult horror film *Rosemary's Baby* and had a history of celebrity tenants. Judy Garland, who played Dorothy in *The Wizard of Oz*, had once lived there.

IN THE FALL of 1974, when John was back in New York and living in a rented apartment, the song "Whatever Gets You Thru the Night," from his new solo album, *Walls and Bridges*, became a No. 1 hit. He had been having such uneven success with his post-Beatles records that he never thought the song would hit it big. For this reason, he had made a promise to his friend Elton John, who had played piano and sung backup vocals on the track: If the song climbed to the top of the charts, he would join Elton onstage. On Thanksgiving Day, John reluctantly but loyally fulfilled his promise to his friend—"It wasn't like I promised some agent or something." He shocked the audience at Madison Square Garden when he came out and performed not only the hit single with Elton but also a couple of Beatles tunes. He hadn't been expecting the crowd to go berserk, but it did.

He also wasn't expecting Yoko to be in the audience. After she had been tipped off that John would be performing, Yoko had asked Elton, who had remained friends with both artists, not to tell John that she would be there. All John knew was that Yoko wished him well: Before the show she had sent him and Elton each a gardenia boutonniere, which the men wore onstage.

Obviously, she wasn't there for the music. "Everybody was applauding like crazy—the house *shook* when [John] came on—and he was there bowing, but that's not what I saw," Yoko said later. "Somehow he looked very lonely to me and I began crying . . . It hit me that he was a very lonely person up onstage there. And he needed me. It was like my soul suddenly saw his soul. So I went backstage."

She found John in his dressing room. He hadn't laid eyes on Yoko in a year, and the sight of her—composed but clearly happy to see him—moved him deeply. The feeling was mutual. "There was just that moment when we saw each other," he said, "and it's like in the movies, you know, when time stands still?"

They began dating, and Yoko gradually decided that she was ready to get back together with John. She had never doubted her love for him, but loving John came with a price. He knew it too. "She had to make the choice whether it was worth lettin' me back in," he said, "not just me but with this mythology that comes with me."

The reconciliation seemed to launch a pair of charmed events. On October 7, 1975, the U.S. Court of Appeals overturned John's deportation order, thanks to Leon Wildes's years of persistence. The court wrote that "Lennon's four-year battle to remain in our country is a testimony to his faith in this American dream." And on October 9, John's thirty-fifth birthday, he received a showstopping gift. Yoko gave birth to their son, Sean Taro Ono Lennon. Fittingly enough, the couple asked Elton John to be the baby's godfather.

About the birth, John told the press, "I feel higher than the Empire State Building," and about becoming a parent with Yoko, he said, "We were finally unselfish enough to want to have a child." Yoko, too, was ecstatic, but she, like John, knew that having a child hadn't been a simple matter of agreeing to do so. They had had several miscarriages over the course of their relationship and had been told by doctors that they could never have children together. For Yoko, the fact that she had Sean at forty-two—an age when any woman might face a real challenge trying to have a baby—seemed like proof that she and John were meant to be, and stay, together.

The "great triple event," as John put it—the Court of Appeals' decision, Sean's birth, and his own birthday—could

OPPOSITE At home in the Dakota with Sean Taro Ono Lennon in 1975. Yoko and John wanted their child's name to reflect both sides of his heritage: "Sean" is the Irish version of "John," and "Taro" is a Japanese name meaning "firstborn male son." "John and I wanted Sean to be as international as possible," Yoko said.

have inspired a rejuvenated Yoko and John to renew their very public championship of peace, social justice, and edgy art. The fact that in April the last U.S. Marines had been brought home from Vietnam, a war widely considered the United States' first defeat, didn't mean that the universe was at peace, and the artists certainly wanted the best world possible for their child. But instead of making statements through megaphones or on record albums, they did something so out of character that it surprised even them: They completely retreated from the limelight.

"Walking away is much harder than carrying on," John insisted. But it also meant the end of pressure to meet recording-contract deadlines and produce gold-standard music. Four months after Sean's birth, John let his recording contract expire. Just as Yoko had supported him when he decided to try to be something more than a Beatle, she supported him when he realized that he didn't even have to be a musician if he didn't feel like it. He wanted to try what he called "real life."

But no one could accuse Yoko and John of selling out by becoming a conventional family: It was Yoko who left home every day to tend to business, and it was John who, with some help from a nanny, stayed home and took care of Sean. "I did it to experience what it was like being the women who've done it for me," he said. He was speaking of Aunt Mimi, who had raised him, and his other aunts, who had doted on him because his parents, for their own reasons, would not.

The more the couple thought about reversing roles, the more it made sense. "If a father raises the child and a mother carries it, the responsibility is shared," Yoko pointed out. It was also true that losing Kyoko, who hadn't surfaced since Tony took off with her in 1971, had been exquisitely painful, and

Yoko was wary of becoming too attached to another child. "I thought, never again [would I] create a relationship that's so strong that it would affect my life when I lose it."

Even while pregnant with Sean, Yoko was working as John's business manager. This meant handling his post-Beatles catalog of music and representing John whenever it was time to license a Beatles song. Her unexpected genius for investments—maybe Eisuke's banking prowess had rubbed off on his daughter?—allowed the artists to feel comfortable donating 10 percent of their earnings to charity. But they were

Sean and his parents in Japan in 1979. Yoko and John would take him to Japan so that he could get to know Yoko's family. The artists wanted Sean to be proud of his heritage, but they were committed to raising him in New York and not in Japan or England, where they experienced more prejudice as a mixed-race couple.

no longer publicly linked with political causes—as Yoko put it, "We don't wave flags anymore." Still, their domestic arrangement was revolutionary. "John was Mr. Mom and Yoko the feminist CEO, way before these were accepted alternatives," the journalist David Sheff noted. "They set an example that changed the lives of many men and women."

The couple's role reversal got a few bad reviews too. Yoko should have figured that some people would accuse her of reducing John Lennon to being his son's "nanny." The artists thought that these cynics were only proving their point: Why was it beneath a man's dignity but not a woman's to devote his life to caring for a child?

When Yoko was working, John loved to traipse around the neighborhood with bundle-of-energy Sean. Although John would be recognized even in a scarf-and-hat disguise, he was greeted not with the mad, body-tipping rush that he had known as a Beatle in England but with "How are you?" and "How's the baby?" It was the life he had thought he could never have back.

Regardless of what anyone thought of their domestic setup, the artists were going to stick with it. It was working for them—and for Sean. He was, Yoko and John felt, their finest collaboration. Eisuke had died two weeks after Sean's birth and had never met his grandson, but Isoko enjoyed getting to know the funny but levelheaded boy when his parents took him to visit her in Japan. Sean did have more extravagant playthings than the average kid—a large trampoline sat in the family's dining room—but John defended his tendency to materially indulge his son. "I'm giving him all the crap while he's young," he said, "so that by the time he's ten, this kind of stuff won't mean anything to him. He'll have had his fix." Yoko left the matter to John. After all, he was doing a terrific job taking care of their son while she was at work downstairs at Studio One, the business office she had set up on the Dakota's ground floor.

Since Sean's birth John hadn't made any music that he shared with the public. Likewise, Yoko hadn't made any art that she presented to the art world, although her work continued to be shown and performed by others. She missed making art, but there would be time for that. And if she made art now, and John had to go back to work to make money, he couldn't be there for Sean. They were fulfilled—to the disappointment of some members of the public, who missed them.

OPPOSITE Yoko and John leaving the Dakota on August 4, 1980, the first day of the *Double Fantasy* recording sessions.

Not that they intended to go on like this forever. In the spring of 1980, when John and Sean were vacationing in Bermuda (Yoko had stayed home to tend to business), John and his assistant decided to check out a local dance club. When John walked in he heard, for the first time, "Rock Lobster," a big hit by the band the B-52s. Like other new-wave artists who were popular at the time, the B-52s made catchy pop music that featured synthetic bursts of noise and quirky vocals. The imitations of imagined fish noises in "Rock Lobster" struck John as uncannily familiar. The disc jockey who had said about *Yoko Ono/Plastic Ono Band* in 1970 that "in 1980 music will probably sound like this" had gotten it right.

John telephoned Yoko from Bermuda and told her that the world had finally caught up with her. He pitched the idea of the two of them making another album together—"They're ready for you this time, kid." Yoko wasn't sold. It was him, not her, she insisted, that the public wanted to hear from after their years of silence. But John wouldn't consider making the album without her.

She *was* intrigued by the idea of creating and recording music again, so she gave in. The couple called the result, released in the fall of 1980, *Double Fantasy*. It was named for a stunning flower that John had seen in a botanical garden in Bermuda. The freesia's two distinct but united colors reminded him of his relationship with Yoko.

The artists were known for making statements to the world, but *Double Fantasy*'s statement wasn't political. It was a proclamation of their deep and tireless affection for each other a dozen years since they first fell in love. They wanted the record's fourteen tracks, which alternate between Yoko's and John's songs, to come across as a dialogue between two lovers.

Yoko and John at the recording studio the Hit Factory in 1980. They wanted their songs on *Double Fantasy* to alternate, like a dialogue. While many of his songs were loving tributes to Yoko and Sean, hers tended to be more hard-hitting. John called "Kiss Kiss Kiss," Yoko's edgy disco song, "vaudeville punk."

Gone was their standard album credit to the Plastic Ono Band. Yoko and John weren't the only musicians on *Double Fantasy*, but as the title they chose suggested, this wasn't really a group effort. For the record's cover, they went with simplicity itself: a close-up black-and-white photo of themselves kissing. *After all these years*, they were saying, *we're back to tell you that this is what it's all about.*

Double Fantasy was hardly the commercially doomed product that was 1972's *Some Time in New York City*, the couple's previous collaborative album. Yoko and John had a newfound appreciation for the pop song. "Pop music is the people's form," Yoko explained. "If I want to communicate with people, I should use their language. Pop songs are that language." And she acknowledged that she had been shooting for a hit record this time, especially for John's sake: "He's used to being No. 1, you know."

The artists had grown accustomed to bad, even mean-spirited reviews of their music: Yoko would bear the brunt, but John, the perceived dupe, would hardly get off easy. So they delighted in the generally positive reviews that *Double Fantasy* was getting—and were somewhere between stunned and flabbergasted that Yoko's songs were being singled out as the more compelling.

Critics felt that Yoko was coming into her own as a songwriter. Her contributions were solidly crafted and reflected her many influences in an appealing and accessible way. She couldn't believe it when seventeen-year-old Julian Lennon told her that most of his friends were buying *Double Fantasy* for "Kiss Kiss Kiss," her hard-edged dance song. The record's critical and popular acceptance helped color Yoko's outlook. She felt certain that the 1980s would be "a marvelous age. We're going to be closer together . . . I *feel* it. It will be beautiful."

The artists had an album's worth of songs left over from the *Double Fantasy* recording sessions, and they were excited about making another record together. On the night of December 8, 1980, they finished recording Yoko's pulsating "Walking on Thin Ice," which they intended for the follow-up album. They both felt great about the song. John told Yoko that it was going to be her first No. 1 hit.

It was nearly eleven P.M. when the limousine bringing them home from the recording studio pulled up in front of the Dakota. Even though they were exhausted, Yoko and John had asked their driver, as they often did, to drop them off on the sidewalk. They preferred to walk, like regular people, rather than be driven into the Dakota's courtyard. This was, in John's phrase, "real life."

As the couple was strolling toward the courtyard, a psychologically unstable young man, who had asked for and received John's autograph earlier that day, shot him multiple times. When the police car that John was riding in arrived at Roosevelt Hospital ten minutes later, he was dead. ▪

8

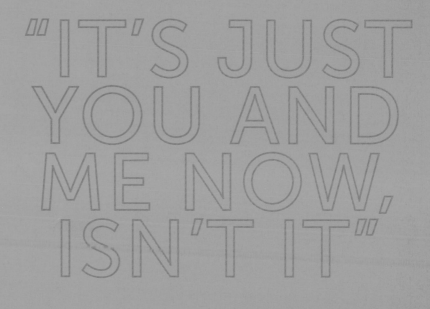

"IT'S JUST YOU AND ME NOW, ISN'T IT"

(1980–1994)

" He's still with us . . .
You can't kill a person that easily. "

—YOKO ONO, 1984

When the world got word that John had been killed, fans gathered outside the Dakota by the hundreds. To keep them at bay, police erected barricades in front of the building's entrance on West Seventy-second Street. The mourners sobbed and held up handmade tribute signs. One featured a photograph of John flanked by two peace symbols above the word WHY? That said it all.

Into the night the mourners sang along with the radio, which played "Imagine," "All You Need Is Love," and other John Lennon songs that now seemed almost unbearably idealistic, considering how he had died. For Yoko, whose bedroom faced West Seventy-second Street, "it was torture. I sent an assistant down to beg them to stop it, but . . . at the same time . . . what if nobody had been there—how would I have felt?"

She couldn't bring herself to tell five-year-old Sean what had happened until a couple of days after John's death. When she finally called him into her bedroom and told him, the little boy put on a brave face. But after he left her room, he ran to his bedroom and cried. In the days and weeks that followed, Sean would kid around to try to make his mother feel better. But Yoko's assistants confided in her that when she wasn't around, he wouldn't disguise his true feelings.

Yoko spent the week following John's death in bed. "I couldn't move," she said. "Just going to the bathroom was a big trip." At first she couldn't eat, and when she did it was chocolate cake—John's guilty pleasure. She received some visitors, including a devastated Ringo Starr and a shattered Julian, but overall Yoko preferred to be alone in her grief.

She had John's body cremated, and instead of arranging a funeral, which would have to be closed to the public, she asked that those who wanted to pay their respects spend ten minutes in silent prayer on Sunday, December 14, at two P.M. New York time. Hundreds of disc jockeys around the world took part in the vigil, broadcasting ten minutes of pure silence. Groups of thousands gathered in cities across the nation, but the largest vigil, with a turnout of more than one hundred thousand, took place in Central Park. The crowd sang "Give Peace a Chance" before turning silent, like millions of others worldwide, for ten minutes. *Rolling Stone* founder Jann Wenner, who was there, saw the irony of this vigil for a slain pacifist icon: "There was, for those ten minutes, world peace."

During the prayer, Yoko was home at the Dakota, well aware of the people congregated below. She released a statement to the media afterward.

> Bless you for your tears and prayers.
> I saw John smiling in the sky.
> I saw sorrow changing into clarity.
> I saw all of us becoming one mind.
> Thank you.

She had always used her work to try to instill hope, but this was the most difficult message of hope that she had ever had to put together.

How could it have happened? How could John Lennon, only forty years old, have become a casualty of the very violence that he had spent so much of his life crusading against? Yoko pondered and pondered the question. "Both of us had been leading a very quiet life, and we suddenly became public. So there was that feeling in the air, that sort of electric feeling, that we were visible again." In her search for answers, Yoko found it tempting to blame John and herself: "Maybe we were too exclusive of our relationship . . . John used to say, 'We don't need *any friends*! We're so self-sufficient! It's great, and it's never boring, it's fantastic . . .' Literally, we didn't socialize at all, and that created some kind of tension and hatred from other people, and we just laughed at that. But when I think about it now . . ."

Suddenly *everybody* wanted to be Yoko's friend. With John gone, the public saw Yoko Ono, its longtime scapegoat, in a new light. Overnight she became someone considered worthy of the world's sympathy. Condolence notes flooded the Dakota. Yoko's reaction was mixed. "I want to say, 'What is this weird behavior? Suddenly you're loving me—and for what? *I* haven't changed.'"

So much had changed with John's death, but Yoko's environment wasn't about to. To the surprise of many, she decided to continue living at the Dakota. It was painful, of course, to be constantly reminded of John—by his possessions, by mementos and souvenirs of their dozen years together. What's more, every time Yoko left or returned home, she had to pass the very spot where her husband had been gunned down before her eyes. But their home was all that Yoko and Sean had left of John, so they stayed.

TWO NIGHTS AFTER John died, Yoko wrote the words to a song about missing someone who is suddenly no longer around. Again and again over the years she had turned to her work for both meaning and reassurance, and it proved to be the one thing that could pull her out of bed after losing John. Within a few weeks of his death, Yoko managed to attend a Beatles-related business meeting. She also began editing music videos for John's *Double Fantasy* song "Woman"—his valentine to her—and for her forthcoming single, "Walking on Thin Ice." It was the song that she and John had just finished recording the night he was killed—he was holding the tape when he was shot.

Yoko also returned to the recording studio. "I really felt that I had almost an uncontrollable anger in me. And I felt that I really needed to do something about it. Otherwise it would eat me up. I felt a desperate need to transform that energy into creativity." But she didn't feel that she was there just for herself. She and John had been "a working team. So it was almost like in the battlefield, and suddenly your friend dies right in front of you, and you have to carry on fighting."

"Season of Glass was the salvation for me," Yoko said of her 1981 album. "I had gone into an uncharted period in my life, with no reference points . . . Music was the most natural thing I could think of. It was part of our life." The album's cover is a photo of John's blood-spattered glasses. As painful as it was to take the photo, Yoko knew that only she could "get it right."

SEASON OF GLASS
YOKO ONO

In the studio Yoko made *Season of Glass*, an album about navigating grief and loss. It includes the hard-driving "I Don't Know Why"—the song that she had written alone in her bedroom two nights after John's death. The bulk of the record's songs are melodic, short, and sung in a straightforward way. "To communicate my feelings sincerely was the most important thing," Yoko said. "Sincere feelings are usually best expressed with simple gestures." Not that the record doesn't have rough edges. "When I recorded 'Goodbye Sadness,' you can hear my voice cracking left and right because it was hard to cut the past. With an engineer's help, I tried to fix it up. But when I heard the smooth version, it was a stranger's voice. So I thought, well, it's hard to say good-bye, anyway. So what if it's cracking?"

Season of Glass, which she released in June 1981, got fine reviews and sold well, but this wasn't Yoko's prize. When she was making the record, Sean would visit her in the studio, and the two would hang out together—something that they had done little of up until this point. The hard truth was, Yoko didn't know her son very well. When John was alive, she would return to the apartment after a long day of work, give Sean a kiss, and then ask him about his day—like a stereotypical dad. With John gone, Yoko and Sean had to get to know each other in a completely different way. "Because John was so close to Sean," Yoko said, "I thought, 'Without John, we're not a family anymore.'" But she and John had worked so hard to redefine what a family was—what was to say she couldn't do it again? And it wasn't exactly a choice. "After John's death I faced this little thing looking at me: 'Oh. It's just you and me now, isn't it.' I had to create a relationship."

For Yoko, life was hardest when she wasn't working or with

Sean. She wrote a lot, as she always had, and she took walks in Central Park and around the city. Now instead of being accompanied by John, she was more often than not accompanied by a bodyguard. Even then, she felt uneasy and found herself looking over her shoulder. But it got better: "Well, maybe I could go to a coffee shop. And then I thought, 'I could possibly even go to the theater.' And slowly I worked my way back into the world."

Traditionally, Japanese women cut their hair following a tragic event, and Yoko had hers snipped into a layered, mid-length style. But she wanted her hair to be as much a symbol of a new chapter in her life as a sign of grief. Working behind outsize dark glasses—like the bags she used to climb into, they allowed her to see out, but no one could see in—Yoko got busy. She released another pop-oriented album, *It's Alright (I See Rainbows)*, in 1982. "In a way," she wrote, "the *It's Alright* time was much more difficult for me . . . than when I had made *Season of Glass*. Life went on. I had to walk and talk normally, while I knew that somewhere inside me there was a clock that had stopped in '80."

Life did go on. It had to—for Sean's sake as well as Yoko's. She even had a new man in her life: a tall Hungarian designer and art dealer named Sam Havadtoy. Sam was a behind-the-scenes fixture in the New York art world and a champion of her work. He lived with Yoko and Sean at the Dakota, and to Yoko's great relief, he and Sean adored each other. Sam would never be John, but at least now the boy had a father figure in his life. Yoko didn't want a new husband, though: "I'm not interested in having a big, smashing romance of the sort of involvement I had with John, and I don't know if I ever will be. That relationship never waned."

While Yoko worked, Sean was in school or in a nanny's care. Many of his classmates also had nannies, but unlike them, Sean had bodyguards. Since John's death, the boy had had dreams about getting shot. Sometimes he dreamed that *Yoko* got shot. After what had happened to his father, Sean understood why his mother insisted that he have bodyguards, but they still took some getting used to. They even escorted him to the bathroom at school.

In many ways, though, Sean was every bit the typical kid. Like his friends, he enjoyed trying to get a rise out of the adults in his life. Unfortunately for him, Yoko wasn't easily shocked. "When I was seven," Sean recalled, "I said, 'Mom, I'm going to get a mohawk.' And she's like, 'Great.' 'No, I'm gonna get a *mohawk*. That means I'm going to shave my head.' And she goes, 'Yeah, yeah, that's great.' Then I didn't do it. I was probably bluffing, anyway. But the fact that she said, 'Great,' it was like, 'Man, I can't do anything to rebel against her.'"

WHEN YOKO LEAST expected it, she received an irresistible invitation. She was asked to participate in a group show at the Chicago Art Fair in 1987 to celebrate her old New York art-world friend John Cage's seventy-fifth birthday. Her contribution, she decided, would be simultaneously old and new. She created a bronze version of a 1966 piece called *White Chess Set*, renaming it the more inviting *Play It By Trust*. The piece is a chess set—sort of. The board and chess pieces are made of bronze and painted white. Since each player's pieces are indistinguishable from his or her opponent's, when two people sit down to play chess, it's impossible to keep track of whose pieces are whose after only a few moves. No one wins, and no one loses.

With the look-alike game pieces, many representing people, Yoko was revisiting a favorite theme: the underlying similarities among all human beings. She was also using *Play It By Trust* to ask players to question the value of competition. "It's confusing—which one is yours," she wrote. "And you start to really understand that it doesn't matter. We're together. We're on the same side. You realize that it's not important to win."

Museumgoers were taken with *Play It By Trust*. So were museum curators. Yoko was invited to mount a solo show at New York's Whitney Museum of American Art. The last high-profile exhibition of her visual art had been her *This Is Not Here* retrospective in 1971; 1989's *Yoko Ono: Objects, Films* was, in many critics' opinions, long overdue.

Play It By Trust (1986–1987) is a chess set that's entirely white, though cast in bronze. As the game proceeds, it's increasingly difficult for players to keep track of their game pieces. With *Play It By Trust*, Yoko is asking, Is competition necessary? And if we can't compete, would that be the end of conflict?

Recasting her *White Chess Set* in bronze had been so satisfying that Yoko was inspired to do the same with more than a dozen other pieces. She called this her Bronze Age series, and this time she didn't cover up the bronze with white paint. The instruction *Painting to Hammer a Nail* and the object *Eternal Time* got the bronze treatment. By bronzing *Apple*, Yoko was, in a way, immortalizing the bite that John had taken out of the apple at her Indica Gallery show the day they met. She knew that bronzing her art didn't just change its look: It changed the work's meaning. Approachable-looking objects that had once practically begged to be touched were suddenly pricey-looking, austere, even intimidating. As with bagism, Yoko was challenging viewers to consider what's beneath the surface. When things (and people) *look* different, are they *really* different?

Something incredible was happening. The interest in Yoko's art, nudged by the Whitney exhibition, was mounting. Invitations to show her work started rolling in. Over the next half-dozen years she had solo exhibitions in cities from London to Tokyo, Berlin to Budapest. Film retrospectives of her work played in New York, Boston, and elsewhere. *Yoko Ono: Arias and Objects*, a book assessing her art, was published. Yoko was at once thrilled and humbled by the attention. Her art was getting a second life. This was something that she knew rarely happened in the often famous-for-just-a-day art world—fame for "fifteen minutes," as Andy Warhol had put it.

By the early 1990s, conceptualism was experiencing a renaissance in popularity. And performance art—what Yoko and her friends had called events—had become the art world's big thing. Many conceptual and performance artists, especially women, owed a debt to Yoko and said so. Innovative women were becoming reliable, in-the-foreground presences in the art world. It was about time.

Women were also making themselves known in the rock music world. With Yoko's enthusiastic consent, the all-female Los Angeles punk band L7 sampled some of her vocals from the Plastic Ono Band's 1969 debut in Toronto. Yoko had unintentionally inspired other rock acts as well, including Barenaked Ladies, who released a tongue-in-cheek love song called "Be My Yoko Ono" that became a hit. These tributes got Yoko thinking. If her art was getting a second life, what kind of reaction would her old music get? In 1992 she released *Onobox*, a six-CD collection of her music, which was largely out of print. The American music-industry magazine *Billboard* called its songs "musically years ahead of their time."

Yoko was as busy as she had ever been, and her mind wasn't as focused on John as it had been in the years immediately following his death. But even with Sam on the scene, she couldn't banish to the history books what had been the love affair of her life. She wrote a musical called *New York Rock* that was more than loosely based on her life with John. Still, she gave the main characters the generic names Bill and Jill so that theatergoers would understand that *New York Rock* could be anyone's story.

For its music, Yoko wrote some new songs but mainly borrowed from her back catalog. When *New York Rock* played Off-Broadway in the spring of 1994, it was well received by theatergoers and critics, as well as by its composer. Yoko always liked it when her work was performed by others because she felt so strongly that art belongs to everyone.

But at least one person wasn't all that impressed by the production, with its slick arrangements typical of musicals. Sean, by this point a solid guitarist, found himself missing his mom's less conventional approach to music. He convinced Yoko to record the raw album *Rising*, which would come out the following year, with his own band. He and his bandmates were honored that Yoko, who could have hired more polished and experienced musicians, wanted to work with a bunch of, well, kids. Boosted by Sean's vote of confidence, Yoko, now sixty-one years old, set out to make music her way—the old way.

Not many of *Rising*'s songs would have made it onto the pop albums Yoko put out in the 1980s. "Warzone" could pass as a hardcore-punk song. "Ask the Dragon" shifts back and forth between funky and tripped out. In "Will I," the vocals are spoken, not sung, and the instruments are subdued to an atmospheric background din. Yoko's screams, shrieks, and wails on the record came easily to her and from a very primal place.

By returning to her old singing style, Yoko wasn't taking a walk down memory lane. Since she had been ahead of her time, as many rock critics, musicians, and fans had come to decide, "then" was now. And she had never looked more contemporary. She had had her layered hairstyle of the 1980s cut into short black spikes. She favored black clothing, but not in the loose-fitting beat style of her Sarah Lawrence days: Her jeans and tops now showed off a figure that not many expected of someone in her sixties. And while Yoko still wore dark glasses, she had exchanged her large frames for smaller ones. When she spoke or listened, she often looked over her lenses and directly at whomever she was speaking to. Fourteen years later, the pain of losing John was still there, but Yoko was finally ready to let the world back in. ∎

ABOVE Yoko loved playing music with Sean, and not just because she got to spend loads of time with him: She was awed by his musical talent.

9

MEND PIECE

(1994–PRESENT)

" When I became seventy, something happened in my brain, like—wow, great! "

—YOKO ONO, 2005

Prompted by *Rising*'s unexpected critical success, Yoko agreed to support the album with a tour. The receptions were all great, and she loved playing with Sean night after night because she valued his company and musicianship and also because he understood her. "I felt that Sean was very supportive of me, just like John," she said. "So there were no sort of silly questions, you know, like 'Why are you screaming, Yoko?'"

Things were going Yoko's way: She had a new generation of fans, a close companion in Sam, and a son who liked creating challenging music with her. She also had something that had been missing from her life for more than two decades.

In 1994, Yoko hadn't seen Kyoko since 1971, when the girl was not yet eight. The last time Yoko had spoken with her was in 1979, when the teenager had phoned her mother out of the blue. All Kyoko had wanted was to make a connection, and Yoko was deeply grateful.

During that phone call, Kyoko said that she would visit, and Yoko was cautiously hopeful that she would. But it would be more than a year before Yoko heard from Kyoko again, when she and Tony sent a telegram of condolence upon learning of John's death. After another year went by, Yoko was still harboring a hope that her daughter would make her way to the Dakota. "When she comes out, I will tell her straight the kind of life I had and what happened," Yoko told *Rolling Stone*. "Despite the fact that I wasn't tying her shoelaces during the years we were together, we had a buddy-buddy relationship and I'm sure she missed me as a mother." But Kyoko didn't come for the promised visit.

Yoko went on with her life, but in 1986 she received shocking news: Tony had given an interview to *People* magazine. In it, he revealed that he and Kyoko had spent some of the years hiding from Yoko and John in a religious cult, known as the Walk, in California. To young Kyoko, hiding had made sense: She had no way of knowing that her mother just wanted to see her and wasn't trying to have Tony put in jail for kidnapping. "It was very painful losing my mom," Kyoko said later, "but I love my dad too . . . I was protective."

After she and Tony left the Walk, in 1977, they stayed in Los Angeles, where Kyoko attended high school under an assumed name—one of nine she used over the years. She had been through a lot in her short life, but somehow she had come through it all a strong and clear-thinking young woman. As for Tony, the years had mellowed him on the subject of Kyoko reuniting with her mother. With hindsight, he could see that Yoko had suffered during the custody battle as much as he had. But it no longer mattered what he thought about his daughter's relationship—if there was even going to be one—with Yoko: Kyoko was an adult now.

When *People* contacted Yoko for a response to Tony's interview, she was blindsided. There were so many different ways to respond. She could play it cool and make a simple statement to the reporter about her relief at learning that Kyoko was doing well. She could vent her anger toward her ex-husband for taking her daughter away. She could share with the public her version of what had happened all those years ago. Instead, she replied with an open letter—not to Tony, but to her daughter.

Dear Kyoko,

All these years there has not been one day I have not missed you. You are always in my heart. However, I will not make any attempt to find you now as I wish to respect your privacy. I wish you all the best in the world. If you ever wish to get in touch with me, know that I love you deeply and would be very happy to hear from you. But you should not feel guilty if you choose not to reach me. You have my respect, love, and support forever.

Love, Mommy

Kyoko didn't respond to the letter. She still didn't feel ready to see her mother, but she found herself fantasizing about getting to know her again. It had been hard to know her even before Tony took her away, because Yoko had become a public figure, and John, who was always sweet and kind to Kyoko, could be "this consuming force," Kyoko said. "He wanted all of my mom, and there wasn't a lot of her left for me." And to young Kyoko, Yoko and John's fame was "a drag. Everywhere you went, people were, you know, screaming."

Eight years after she first read Yoko's open letter to her, Kyoko felt ready to talk to her mother. In 1994, Kyoko's life was full—she was married and a practicing social worker living in Colorado—but she knew that there was some unfinished business to take care of. "When I became engaged, I told my husband that before I have children I will want to contact my mother. I just don't feel it's right for me to become a mother without at least letting my mother know that I'm alive and well. And so I called her up."

Although Yoko had always been optimistic, by 1994 she had practically resigned herself to the idea that she had lost her daughter for good. Yet she continued to hold on to a thread of hope. After the *People* magazine story came out, every time Kyoko's birthday rolled around, Yoko placed an advertisement in newspapers wishing her a happy birthday and appealing to her to get in touch if and when she felt ready. Hearing from

Kyoko now, it was as if Yoko had asked for the moon and was given the moon and the stars combined.

Kyoko wasn't just thinking about her own feelings when she suggested a get-together. She had begun to realize that a meeting was essential to her mother's healing process, as well as to her own. The reunion, which took place in New York in late 1994, was just that: healing. "When Kyoko appeared finally, I was totally in shock," Yoko said. "It felt like the part of me that was missing came back." And this time, after a twenty-three-year absence, Kyoko was back in her life for good.

OVER THE NEXT several years, while Yoko was juggling multiple commitments to exhibit her work and play her music, she was also giving a lot of her time to a woman named Alexandra Munroe. A longtime fan of Yoko's art, Munroe was the director of the Japan Society, for which Yoko and Toshi had worked decades earlier. Munroe had first contacted Yoko in 1995, when she had had an idea: She wanted to organize a retrospective of Yoko's work. It would be Yoko's first since the Everson Museum of Art had put on *This Is Not Here* more than two decades before.

Yoko's initial reaction wasn't a feeling of pride but of wariness. The idea of a retrospective hadn't bothered her when she was in her thirties, when she had felt as though she might live forever. But now that she was in her sixties, the idea grated. Weren't retrospectives for artists her age a way of saying that their best work was behind them? But after giving the matter some thought, she came around. A retrospective guaranteed a large audience for her art, and Yoko was all for that.

The forty-year retrospective, which Alexandra Munroe co-curated with Yoko's Fluxus comrade Jon Hendricks, who had become a scholar of the art group, opened in October 2000 at

Sean, Yoko, and Kyoko together in 1994.

Manhattan's Japan Society Gallery. Yoko had titled the show *YES YOKO ONO* because she wanted to emphasize the "think positive" message that she put in almost all of her work. "There were many incredible negative elements in my life, and in the world, and because of that I had to conjure up a positive attitude within me in balance to the most chaotic," she said. "And I had to balance that by activating the 'yes' element." Naturally, *Ceiling Painting (YES Painting)*, which had changed John Lennon's life, was front and center in the show.

YES YOKO ONO got rave reviews and attracted droves of viewers. It featured nearly one hundred and fifty works of art. A favorite was 1996's *Wish Tree*. Viewers were invited to write their wishes on small cards and tie them to the branches of an actual potted tree. This way, people were joining together their hopes and dreams, which Yoko felt gave the wishes more power. The idea had come straight from her childhood in Japan. "I used to go to a temple and write out a wish on a piece of thin paper and tie it in a knot around the branch of a tree," she explained. "Trees in temple courtyards were always filled with people's wish knots, which looked like white flowers blossoming from afar." She didn't read the wishes that accumulated at her retrospective: She considered them too private. Besides, what they said wasn't the point. "In the end, I'm going to collect all the wishes, without reading them, and put it in one big . . . container and make it into a sculpture of wishes."

YES YOKO ONO won awards and would travel around the world over the next several years. The art critic Arthur C. Danto, who called Yoko "one of the most original artists of the last half-century," was speaking for others who were now viewing her work in a new light when he said, "Her fame made her almost impossible to see."

OPPOSITE Yoko performing with IMA—Sean is on the left—in New York in 1996. She was thrilled that his generation was connecting with her music. About *Rising*, *Spin* magazine wrote, "Yoko Ono turns . . . noises into terrible, beautiful music." Yoko could hardly believe it. When *Yoko Ono/Plastic Ono Band* came out, no one was calling it "beautiful." Some weren't even calling it "music."

LEFT On September 15, 2003, Yoko performed *Cut Piece* at the Théâtre du Ranelagh in Paris. Although others had done so, Yoko hadn't performed *Cut Piece* since the mid-1960s—a time when, looking back, the world had seemed like a relatively peaceful place. Before the performance began, Yoko said from the stage in French, ". . . Imagine peace. Peace for you and me and all the world. Never forget love . . ."

The success of *YES YOKO ONO* coincided with the end of a phase in her life: In 2000, Yoko and Sam called it quits after nearly twenty years together. Between coming to terms with life without Sam and promoting *YES YOKO ONO* and her new album, *Blueprint for a Sunrise*, Yoko's plate was full. She didn't mind when a project came her way that demanded little of her, as when the Orange Factory, a New York music production company, asked for permission to remix and rerelease her 1971 song "Open Your Box." It became an underground dance-club hit. No one was happier for Yoko than regular dance-hit makers the B-52s. They invited her to join them onstage at New York's Irving Plaza to sing "Rock Lobster" at the band's twenty-fifth-anniversary concert in February 2002. Microphone in hand, Yoko had a ball showing everyone how it was done.

A year later Yoko was dancing again, at her seventieth birthday party. Seventy was quite a milestone, but for Yoko this birthday represented an opening in her life, not a closing down. "People think that their world will get smaller as they get older," she said. "My experience is just the opposite."

Rising to the big occasion, Sean organized a mammoth birthday party for Yoko at the New York hot spot Mr. Chow. In addition to her two children, two hundred of Yoko's friends from over the years attended. Guests could climb into—what else?—a large bag, or dance on a giant version of *Painting to Be Stepped On*, while *Bottoms* was projected onto the restaurant's walls. Yoko had the time of her life—her long life. "Something happened to me when I became seventy," she said later. "I started to feel a tremendous love for the human race, and life and this planet, the universe, the whole shebang."

In the past year or so Yoko had become, quite unwittingly, something of a dance-club diva. Suddenly it was open season on her old songs. The DJ Superchumbo had remixed "Kiss Kiss Kiss." The Orange Factory had returned, this time to remix a song called "Yangyang." With two Yoko Ono hits on its hands now, the Orange Factory decided to go for three, this time with "Walking on Thin Ice," the song that Yoko and John had finished the night he was murdered. The song became a No. 1 dance single, even beating out hits by chart toppers Madonna and Justin Timberlake. Yoko joked that she belonged in the book *Guinness World Records*: At seventy, surely she was the oldest person ever to have a No. 1 dance hit. But this time she wasn't completely surprised by the remix's success. John had, in a sense, tipped her off when he predicted that it would be her first No. 1 hit.

Despite the dance-club scene's embrace, Yoko was gradually beginning to realize that she was facing a new kind of prejudice. "It's a very strange situation," she said. "I thought, well, I dealt with sexism and racism, and I did my best, and finally I'm in a position where I don't have to worry so much about it. And then ageism came up, you know? I'm sure most people are the same: You don't really think you're old. But society treats you differently."

And it wasn't that she was feeling old or looking anywhere near her age—quite the opposite. With her strikingly youthful appearance—trim figure, tinted glasses, spiky dark hair accented with maroon or eggplant or streaked with blond—she was challenging stereotypes every time she walked out the door.

TO STAY FIT, Yoko works with a trainer and walks through Central Park—sometimes twice a day. She visits Strawberry Fields, her gift to the park: a 2.5-acre teardrop-shaped oasis named for one of the most cherished Beatles-era John Lennon songs. (Yoko can see Strawberry Fields from her window at the Dakota.) Her brisk pace is partly because there's so much she wants to do and partly in order to pass by unnoticed. "Perhaps people think it is morbid, me still living here," she said. "They look up to my window and think, oh, she's right up there. While they're looking up, that's when I go by, very quickly."

Yoko thrives on a high-octane schedule. "I'm excited and interested every day of my life," she said. "I don't tell myself, 'Oh, it's twelve midnight, so I better go to sleep.' Things happen, and I just go with it." She knows she's a workaholic, and she doesn't apologize for it. "It's like when you're going somewhere and you only have one suitcase and you want to squeeze everything in there. And you think you can't squeeze everything in there but, voilà!, you can. That's like my day. I try to squeeze everything in."

A steady source of enjoyment is dinners with friends. Yoko likes striking out to restaurants on foot and sometimes hikes a few miles downtown to her beloved Greenwich Village to see Sean, who has a home there. She travels a lot to promote her work, which continues to be exhibited around the globe, and of course she accepted an invitation to speak out for world peace by introducing John's "Imagine" at the opening ceremony of the Winter Olympics in Turin, Italy, in February 2006. And later that year, she went to Iceland to attend a groundbreaking ceremony for IMAGINE PEACE TOWER, which began shining its light on what would have been John's sixty-seventh birthday: October 9, 2007. To date, more than a million *Wish Tree* wishes have been collected, and Yoko hopes to incorporate them into IMAGINE PEACE TOWER one day, making it the "sculpture of wishes" she first dreamed of.

OPPOSITE IMAGINE PEACE TOWER, in Iceland, is Yoko's memorial to John: Every year it shines from October 9—his birthday—through December 8, the day he died.

BELOW Sean, Yoko, former Beatle Ringo Starr, and Olivia Harrison (widow of former Beatle George Harrison) attended the inaugural lighting of IMAGINE PEACE TOWER on October 9, 2007.

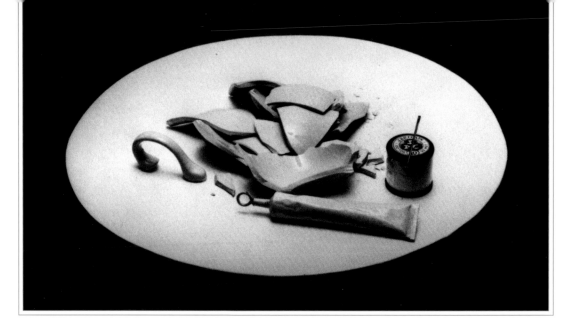

ABOVE Yoko first created *Mend Piece* in 1966 as a sculpture for her Indica Gallery exhibition, and she still performs it with others. What's important, she feels, isn't how well the broken shards are glued together but the idea of healing something—or someone.

OPPOSITE Yoko is still collecting skies.

But for people who consider wishing too abstract, there are always Yoko's mend pieces, which she has performed, and has gotten others to perform with her, over the years. Her mend pieces require taking broken fragments of china and gluing them together, paying little attention to pattern or fit. The point isn't to glue the pieces together cleanly; it's that broken things—and broken relationships and broken hearts—are worth taking the time to repair.

Sean, who still makes music with Yoko, marvels at not only his mother's amazing physical stamina but also her ability to see art everywhere. "If we're driving to a movie theater in a taxi, she'll be like, 'Get me a piece of paper!' And she'll . . . write something down, and a couple of days later it will either be, like, some art piece or a painting or a song, or something."

And why *couldn't* anything be art? And why, Yoko had wondered all her life, did art—or a human being, for that matter—have to fall into a particular category? "There were always people who felt, 'That was very Fluxus,' or 'That was not Fluxus,'" she said. "Or, 'That's not rock.' Or, 'What I thought was poetry, no, that's more like prose.' Something maybe doesn't fit, but that part is me. You always end up being yourself." ∎

Acknowledgments

We would like to thank the following people for their invaluable contributions to our book: Bill Arning, Ian Ayres, DJ Spooky, Eden Edwards, Simone Forti, Paul Goresh, Sari Gurney and Friends of Yoko, Jon Hendricks, Jonas Herbsman, Hiroko Kikuchi, Abby Lester, Albert Maysles, Jonas Mekas, Jeff Perkins, Yvonne Rainer, Jeremy Skaller, Midori Yamamura, Midori Yoshimoto, and Kumiko Yoshioka. We are indebted to the Cambridge Public Library research magicians. We would have been lost without Jim Armstrong, Tamar Brazis, Melissa Faulner, Katherine Fausset, Maria Middleton, Jenna Pocius, and Mary Ann Zissimos. We're beyond grateful for the generosity of Bob Gruen and the help of the angels at Studio One: Andrew Kachel, Amanda Keeley, and Karla Merrifield. And to Yoko, our gratitude is approximately infinite.

Nell would like to thank George Beram, for being a hippie (at least for a while); Gillie Campbell, for indulging her stepdaughter's Yoko habit; Joe Klompus, for outsmarting the Genius Bar; and the late Judy McConnell, for burning her bra but not her Beatles records.

Carolyn would like to thank Kim Patch and Jonathan Klausner, for computer magic; Rachel Clark, Caroline Clark, Minona Heaviland, and Lia Barnes Lenart, for help in the early days; Margaret Lacey, JoAnn Hughes, and the late Charlie Weiner, for opening a door back to the Village; "sis" Barbara Epstein, for encouragement and cheers from day one; and Shelly, for his enthusiasm and support for Project Yoko.

TIMELINE

FEBRUARY 18, 1933 | Yoko Ono is born in Tokyo, Japan.

1953 | Yoko enrolls in Gakushūin University as its first female philosophy student. (She drops out after two semesters.)

SUMMER/FALL 1953 | Yoko moves to Scarsdale, New York, to live with her parents and enrolls in Sarah Lawrence College, in Bronxville, New York. (She drops out after her junior year.)

1956 | Yoko elopes with composer Toshi Ichiyanagi. They live in New York City.

FALL 1960 | Yoko and Toshi move to 112 Chambers Street, where she hosts the Chambers Street series.

EARLY 1961 | Yoko and Toshi separate; Toshi moves back to Tokyo.

JULY 1961 | *Paintings and Drawings by Yoko Ono*, Yoko's first visual-art show, opens at AG Gallery, in New York.

MARCH 1962 | Yoko moves back to Tokyo.

MAY 1962 | *Works of Yoko Ono* opens at Sogetsu Art Center, in Tokyo.

1962 | While still in Japan, Yoko meets and becomes romantically involved with New Yorker Tony Cox. (Some months later Yoko and Toshi divorce, and Yoko marries Tony.)

AUGUST 3, 1963 | Kyoko Cox, Yoko and Tony's daughter, is born.

JULY 4, 1964 | Yoko self-publishes *Grapefruit*, her book of poemlike instructions.

SEPTEMBER 1964 | Yoko moves back to New York with Tony and Kyoko.

MARCH 21, 1965 | Yoko performs *Cut Piece* at Carnegie Recital Hall.

EARLY 1966 | Yoko makes the hit underground film *No. 4*, which becomes informally known as *Bottoms*.

SEPTEMBER 1966 | Yoko travels to London with Tony and Kyoko to participate in the Destruction in Art Symposium.

NOVEMBER 1966 | *Unfinished Paintings and Objects by Yoko Ono* opens at Indica Gallery, in London. Yoko meets Beatle John Lennon there.

MAY 1968 | Yoko and John become romantically involved. (Soon afterward, they end their respective marriages.)

MARCH 20, 1969 | Yoko and John wed in Gibraltar.

MARCH 25, 1969 | Yoko and John begin their weeklong honeymoon *Bed-In for Peace* at the Amsterdam Hilton.

MAY 26, 1969 | Yoko and John begin their eight-day *Bed In* at Montreal's Queen Elizabeth Hotel.

FEBRUARY 1970 | A reissue of *Grapefruit* is published by Simon & Schuster.

OCTOBER/DECEMBER 1970 | Yoko records and releases her first solo album, *Yoko Ono/Plastic Ono Band*.

AUGUST 1971 | Yoko and John move to New York.

AUGUST/SEPTEMBER 1971 | Yoko records and releases her album *FLY*.

OCTOBER 9, 1971 | *This Is Not Here*, Yoko's first career retrospective, opens at the Everson Museum of Art, in Syracuse, New York.

SPRING 1973 | Yoko and John move into the Dakota.

FALL 1973 | Yoko and John separate. John goes to California.

THANKSGIVING DAY 1974 | Yoko and John reunite backstage at an Elton John concert at Madison Square Garden.

OCTOBER 9, 1975 | Sean Lennon, Yoko and John's son, is born. Yoko and John settle into "real life."

FALL 1980 | Yoko and John release *Double Fantasy*.

DECEMBER 8, 1980 | John is murdered outside the Dakota.

JUNE 1981 | Yoko releases *Season of Glass*.

OCTOBER 9, 1985 | Strawberry Fields—an international garden of peace in New York's Central Park—is dedicated to John Lennon and opened to the public.

FEBRUARY 1989 | *Yoko Ono: Objects, Films* opens at the Whitney Museum of American Art, in New York.

LATE 1994 | Yoko and Kyoko reunite in New York after a twenty-three-year separation.

JULY 1995 | Yoko and IMA, Sean's band, release *Rising*.

OCTOBER 2000 | *YES YOKO ONO* opens at the Japan Society Gallery, in New York.

OCTOBER 9, 2007 | IMAGINE PEACE TOWER, erected in Iceland, begins shining its light.

JUNE 5, 2009 | Yoko is awarded the Golden Lion for Lifetime Achievement at the 2009 Venice (Italy) Biennale.

BIBLIOGRAPHY

BOOKS

Ayres, Ian. *Private Parts: The Early Works of Ian Ayres*. Paris: French Connection Press, 2005.

Christy, Marian. *Marian Christy's Conversations: Famous Women Speak Out*. Cambridge, Mass.: Lumen Editions, 1998.

Coleman, Ray. *Lennon*. New York: McGraw-Hill, 1984.

Cott, Jonathan, and Christine Doudna, eds. *The Ballad of John and Yoko*. Garden City, N.Y.: Rolling Stone Press, 1982.

Eccher, Danilo, ed. *Yoko Ono: 3 Rooms*. Galleria Civica di Arte catalogue. Milan, Italy: Skira, 1995.

Fawcett, Anthony. *John Lennon: One Day at a Time*. New York: Grove Press, 1976.

Gaar, Gillian G. *She's a Rebel: The History of Women in Rock & Roll*, rev. 2nd ed. New York: Seal Press, 2002.

Godfrey, Tony. *Conceptual Art*. London: Phaidon Press Limited, 1998.

Gordon, Beate Sirota. *The Only Woman in the Room*. New York: Kodansha America, Inc., 2001.

Gruen, Bob. *John Lennon: The New York Years*. New York: Stewart, Tabori & Chang, 2005.

Haskell, Barbara, and John G. Hanhardt, eds. *Yoko Ono: Arias and Objects*. Salt Lake City: Peregrine Smith Books, 1991.

Hopkins, Jerry. *Yoko Ono*. New York: Macmillan Publishing Company, 1986.

Iles, Chrissie. *Yoko Ono: Have You Seen the Horizon Lately?* Exhibition catalog. Oxford: Museum of Modern Art, 1997.

Kane, Larry. *Lennon Revealed*. Philadelphia: Running Press, 2005.

Munroe, Alexandra, and Jon Hendricks. *YES Yoko Ono*. New York: Japan Society and Harry N. Abrams, 2000.

Ono, Yoko. *Grapefruit: A Book of Instructions and Drawings*. New York: Simon & Schuster, 2000.

———. *Instruction Paintings*. New York: Weatherhill, 1995.

Ono, Yoko, ed. *Memories of John Lennon*. New York: HarperEntertainment, 2005.

Partridge, Elizabeth. *John Lennon: All I Want Is the Truth: A Biography*. New York: Viking, 2005.

Prose, Francine. *The Lives of the Muses: Nine Women & the Artists They Inspired*. New York: HarperCollins, 2002.

Saint-Exupéry, Antoine de. *The Little Prince*. New York: Harcourt, Inc., 2000.

Sheff, David, ed. *All We Are Saying: The Last Major Interview with John Lennon and Yoko Ono*. New York: St. Martin's Griffin, 2000; originally published as *The Playboy Interviews with John Lennon and Yoko Ono*. New York: Playboy Press, 1981.

Sumner, Melody, Kathleen Burch, and Michael Sumner, eds. *The Guests Go in to Supper*. San Francisco: Burning Books, 1986.

Wenner, Jann S., ed. *Lennon Remembers: New Edition*. New York: Verso, 2000.

Wiener, Jon. *Come Together: John Lennon in His Time*. New York: Random House, 1984.

Yoshimoto, Midori. *Into Performance: Japanese Women Artists in New York*. Piscataway Township, N.J.: Rutgers University Press, 2005.

PERIODICALS

Barton, Laura. "Age Becomes Her." *Guardian* (Manchester), June 13, 2005.

Benedikt, Michael. "Yoko Notes." *Art & Artists*, January 1972, 26.

Beram, Nell. "YES Yoko Ono at MIT." Press conference, October 19, 2001. Yoko Ono website, http://a-i-u.net/yes_mit_r.html.

Big Issue. "The Ballad of Yoko." October 15–21, 2007, 9.

Boriss-Krimsky, Carolyn. "Multimedia Pioneer: An Interview with Yoko Ono." *Ruminator Review*, Summer 2002, 26.

———. "Yoko Ono: Art of the Mind." *Art New England*, October/November 2001, 26.

Boston Globe. "Yoko Ono's Year Without Lennon." December 8, 1981.

Camhi, Leslie. "Art Eclipsed by Fame." *Village Voice*, November 7, 2000, 77.

Cheng, Scarlet. "In Her Life: Yoko's Art." *Los Angeles Times*, Calendar Section, October 15, 2000, 3.

Clerk, Carol. "Lennon: The Untold Story." *Uncut: Music & Movies*, January 1998, 62.

Crawdaddy. December 5, 1971.

Danto, Arthur C. "Life in Fluxus." *Nation*, December 18, 2000, 34.

Fricke, David. "The Rolling Stone Interview: Sean Lennon." *Rolling Stone*, June 11, 1998, 38.

Gann, Kyle. "The Part That Doesn't Fit Is Me: Yoko Ono: The Inventor of Downtown." *Village Voice*, August 11, 1992, 69.

Gordon, Kim. "Yoko Ono Talks with Kim Gordon: Two Women Ahead of the Avant-Garde." *Interview*, March 2001, 108.

Graustark, Barbara. "Yoko: An Intimate Conversation." *Rolling Stone*, October 1, 1981, 13.

Hertzberg, Hendrik. "Everywhere's Somewhere." *New Yorker*, January 8, 1972, 28.

———. "A Reporter at Large" *New Yorker*, December 9, 1972, 138.

Hinton, Leslie. "An Indignant Protest, So Fragrantly Expressed." *Sun*, March 11, 1967, .

Hooks, Bell. "The Dancing Heart: A Conversation between Yoko Ono and bell hooks." *Paper,* September 1997.

Huston, Johnny. Review of *Rising,* by Yoko Ono, Capitol Records. *Spin,* December 1995, 86.

Jacobson, Mark. "Life with John: The Dakota as Good Memory Motel," *New York,* September 29, 2003, 38.

Kemp, Mark. "She Who Laughs Last: Yoko Ono Reconsidered." *Option,* July/August 1992, 74.

Larocca, Amy. "Yoko, Now: The Surprisingly Sexy Septuagenarian." *New York,* February 14, 2005, 84

Lennon, John. "Lennon Larfs." *Us,* March 17, 1981, 32.

Loder, Kurt. "Yoko Ono: 'Still in a State of Shock.'" *Rolling Stone,* January 20, 1983, 42.

MacSweeney, Eve. "Yoko Rising." *Vogue,* August 2006, 250.

McCarry, Charles. "John Rennon's Excrusive Gloupie." *Esquire,* December 1970, 204.

McFadden-Schroth, Susan. "Yoko Ono: Singing to Give Peace a Chance." *Stripes,* March 6, 1986, 20.

McKenna, Kristine. "Yoko Reconsidered." *Los Angeles Times,* Calendar Section, April 11, 1993, 3.

Mead, Rebecca. "Department of Legacies." *New Yorker,* April 20, 1998, 45

Morse, Steve. "Another Lennon Inspires Ono's Tour." *Boston Globe,* May 8, 1996, 50

Occhiogrosso, Peter. "Yoko Ono in Her Own Words." *Boston Globe,* Calendar Extra, December 11, 1980, 7; adapted from article in *Soho News* (New York, N.Y.), December 3, 1980.

O'Dair, Barbara. "Yoko Ono." *Rolling Stone,* November 13, 1997, 114.

Ono, Yoko. "Feeling the Space," *New York Times,* August 24, 1973.

———. "The Feminization of Society." *New York Times,* February 23, 1972.

———. Interview on WBAI, 1971, quoted in fanzine *Yoko Only* 20 (Autumn 1987).

———. "Of a Grapefruit in the World of Park." *Campus* 26, no. 4 (October 26, 1955).

Payne, John. "O, No! Arthurfest Headliner Yoko Ono on the Beatles, Baseball, Sex and Peace," *LA Weekly,* September 2–8, 2005, 100.

Paytress, Mark. "Yoko Ono: The Mojo Interview." *Mojo,* August 2007, 40.

People. "Oh Yes! Ono Turns 70," March 31, 2003, 97.

———. "Yoko Ono's Ex-Husband, Tony Cox, Reveals His Strange Life Since Fleeing with Their Daughter 14 Years Ago," February 3, 1986, 34.

Pierson, Kate. "The Ballad of Yoko: The B-52's' Kate Pierson Talks with Yoko Ono." *Rolling Stone,* March 19, 1992, 17.

Press, Joy. "Yoko Ono: Mother and Child Reunion." Salon, May 27, 1996 http://salon.com/weekly/tibetlink960527.html.

Robinson, John. "High Concept." *Guardian,* April 23, 2005, 8.

Rollin, Betty. "Top Pop Merger: Lennon/Ono Inc." *Look,* March 18, 1969, 36.

Roth, Katherine. "Yoko's Show Takes Art to Limit." *Chicago Sun-Times,* October 29, 2000, 14.

Seabrook, John. "At Tea: Cognito." *New Yorker,* May 19, 2003, 35.

Sheff-Cahan, Vicki. "A Day in the Life of . . . Yoko Ono." *People,* March 28, 1994, 110.

Smith, Ethan. "He Can Work It Out." *New York,* May 18, 1998, 32.

Tennant, Christopher. "The Onophiles." *New York,* July 15, 2002, 12.

Wasserman, Emily. "This Is Not Here." *Art Forum,* January 1972, 69.

Wilson, Christopher. "Yoko Ono Five Months Later." *Boston Globe,* May 20, 1981.

Yoshimoto, Midori. "Yoko Ono in Conversation with Midori Yoshimoto, February 23, 2001." *Dialogue,* Spring/Summer 2001, 18.

AUDIOVISUAL MATERIALS

Cavett, Dick. *The Dick Cavett Show: John & Yoko Collection.* DVD. Episodes aired September 11, 1971, September 24, 1971, and May 11, 1972. Los Angeles: Shout! Factory LLC, 2005.

Chiaki, Nagano, director. *Some Young People.* Film broadcast as part of Nippon Television's series *Nonfiction Theater* on October 4, 1964. Transcript transcribed, translated, and annotated by Midori Yoshimoto, in Reiko Tomii, ed., "1960s Japan: Art Outside the Box," special issue, *Review of Japanese Culture and Society,* vol. 17 (Dec. 2005), pp. 98–105.

Douglas, Mike. *The Mike Douglas Show with John Lennon & Yoko Ono.* Videocassette (VHS). Episodes aired February 14–18, 1972; accompanying booklet, *The Mike Douglas Show with John Lennon & Yoko Ono,* by Stephen K. Peeples. Burbank, Calif.: Rhino Home Video, 1998.

Egan, Sam, and Andrew Solt. *Imagine: John Lennon.* DVD. Directed by Andrew Solt, 1988. Burbank, Calif.: Warner Home Video, 2005.

Graustark, Barbara. *Yoko Ono (Then and Now).* Videocassette (VHS). Culver City, Calif.: Media Home Entertainment, 1984.

Lennon, John, and Yoko Ono. *Heart Play—Unfinished Dialogue.* Vinyl. New York: PolyGram Records, 1983.

———. *John & Yoko: The Interview.* Audiocassette. Recorded December 6, 1980, with Andy Peebles. London: BBC Enterprises Ltd, 1990.

Lindsay-Hogg, Michael, director. *The Rolling Stones Rock and Roll Circus.* Videocassette (VHS). Originally filmed in 1968. New York: ABKCO, 1996.

Lopez, Thomas. Interview at the Destruction in Art Symposium, Africa Centre, London. Cassette. London, 1966.

Macfarlane, Ursula, director. *The Real Yoko Ono*. London: Channel 4, 2001.

Morris, Robert. Smithsonian Institution Archives of American Art Oral History Program: Interview with Robert Morris. By Paul Cummings. March 10, 1968. One 7-inch soundtape reel, 3:45. http://www.aaa.si.edu/collections/interviews/oral-history-interview-robert-morris-13065.

Ono Lennon, Yoko. "As a Child of Asia." United Nations address, May 4, 2005. Transcript. http://jeclique.com/onoweb/news-un2005.html.

——. *Blueprint for a Sunrise*. Audio CD liner notes. Los Angeles: Capitol, 2001.

——. *Onobox*. Audio CD liner notes. Salem, Mass.: Rykodisc, 1992.

——. *Rising*. Audio CD liner notes. Los Angeles: Capitol, 1995.

——. *Season of Glass*. Vinyl liner notes. New York: Geffen Records, 1981.

Pennebaker, D. A., director. *Sweet Toronto: John Lennon and the Plastic Ono Band*. VHS. Documentary of 1969 Live Peace in Toronto concert. Long Beach, Calif.: Pioneer, 1988.

Reiser, Paul. "Yoko Said." Disc 2. *The Mad About You Collection*. DVD. Directed by David Steinberg, aired November 12, 1995. Culver City, Calif.: Sony Pictures Home Entertainment, 2005.

ORIGINAL INTERVIEWS
conducted by Carolyn Boriss-Krimsky

Arning, Bill. January 23, 2003.

DJ Spooky (Paul D. Miller). March 18, 2005.

Forti, Simone. September 12, 2005.

Hendricks, Jon. April 5, 2001.

Kikuchi, Hiroko. May 7, 2004.

Maysles, Albert. June 9, 2003.

Mekas, Jonas. September 5, 2003.

Ono, Yoko. October 21, 2001.

Perkins, Jeff. July 30, 2005, and September 15, 2005.

Rainer, Yvonne. October 22, 2003.

Skaller, Jeremy. November 30, 2005.

Yamamura, Midori. May 10, 2004.

Yoshimoto, Midori. October 11, 2003, and November 3, 2003.

IMAGE CREDITS

INDEX

Note: Page numbers in italics refer to illustrations.

SEND YOUR WISH TO IMAGINE PEACE TOWER.

Wishing by Mail:
IMAGINE PEACE TOWER
P.O. Box 1009
121 Reykjavík Iceland

Wishing Online:
· On Twitter, by tweeting a direct message to @IPTower
· Via email to wish@IMAGINEPEACETOWER.com
· For more information about IMAGINE PEACE TOWER,
  visit http://IMAGINEPEACETOWER.com

IMAGINA A PAZ

رویای صلح   IMMAGINA LA PACE   חלום שלום

ཞི་བདེ་བསམ།   წარმოიდგინეთ მშვიდობა

BARIŞI DÜŞLE   ILARAWAN ANG MUNDONG MAPAYAPA

평화를 꿈꾸자   IMAGINA LA PAZ

ᓴᐱᓕᖅᑎᑦᑎᓂᖅ   IMAGINE PEACE   احلم سلام

CONTENTS